LEARNING DISABILITY

LEARNING
DISABILITY
The
Unrealized Potential

ALAN O. ROSS

PROFESSOR OF PSYCHOLOGY
STATE UNIVERSITY OF NEW YORK
AT STONY BROOK

McGRAW-HILL BOOK COMPANY

New York   St. Louis   San Francisco   Düsseldorf   London
Mexico   Sydney   Toronto

Library of Congress Cataloging in Publication Data

Ross, Alan O
    Learning disability.

    Bibliography: p.
    Includes index.
    1. Learning disabilities. I. Title.
LC4704.R678   371.9   77-4704
ISBN 0-07-053875-1

123456789   RRDRRD 76543210987

This book was set in Palatino by University Graphics, Inc. It was printed and bound by R. R. Donnelly & Sons Company. The designer was Christine Aulicino. The editors were Thomas Quinn and Cheryl Hanks. Milton Heiberg supervised the production.

TO ILSE
  —for caring

CONTENTS

PREFACE   xiii

Chapter 1. A LEARNING–DISABLED CHILD   1

What Is the Matter with Fred?   1

The Problem and Its Labels   4

   From Dunce to Dyslexia   4

   Why?   6

   What?   7

   Labels and Their Consequences   7

Who Is a Learning-disabled Child?   8

   The Learning-disabled Child Is Not Mentally Retarded   8

   The Learning-disabled Child Is Not Physically Impaired   8

   The Learning-disabled Child Is Not Emotionally Disturbed   9

   The Learning-disabled Child Is Not Culturally Disadvantaged   10

   Who Is a Learning-disabled Child?   11

What about Brain Damage?   12

Chapter 2. HOW DID IT ALL START?   15

A Bit of History   15

   Brain-injured Soldiers   17

   Mentally Retarded Children   19

The Perceptual Motorists   21

The Test Makers   25

Speaking of Language   27

Chapter 3. WHAT IS LEARNING?   29

We All Know What Is Meant by "Learning"   29

   Or Do We?   29

   Learning Is a Concept   31

   Learning Is a Description   31

How Can One Tell that a Child Is Learning?   32

How Can One Tell that a Child Is Not Learning?   36

When Should a Child Be Learning?   37

Potential and Achievement   39

   How Does One Measure Achievement?   42

   A Middle-Class Phenomenon?   43

Chapter 4. IS SOMETHING WRONG WITH THEIR BRAINS?   44

A Futile Assumption   44

   One White Crow   46

   If Not Damage, Then Maybe Dysfunction?   48

What about Hyperactivity?   50

   The Squeaky Wheel   51

   Does It Matter?   53

   What to Do?   54

Drugs and Activity and Learning   55

   Why Do We Know So Little?   55

   What Does It Prove?   56

   What Can One Conclude?   57

Potential Abuses   60

Chapter 5. WHAT CAN ONE TELL FROM TESTS?   61

What Tests Can Do—and What They Cannot Do   61

   Intelligence   64

   Who Is the Average Child?   66

The Wechsler Intelligence Scale for Children—Revised   67

   The Verbal Scale   67

   The Performance Scale   71

The IQ Scores   75

How Fred Did on the WISC-R   75

The Illinois Test of Psycholinguistic Abilities (ITPA)   80

Channels of Communication   81

Levels of Organization   82

Psycholinguistic Processes   82

FUNCTIONS TESTED AT THE AUTOMATIC LEVEL   83

CLOSURE   83

SEQUENTIAL MEMORY   83

FUNCTIONS TESTED AT THE REPRESENTATIONAL
LEVEL   84

RECEPTIVE PROCESS   84

ORGANIZING PROCESS   84

EXPRESSIVE PROCESS   85

What Can the ITPA Tell Us?   86

The ITPA Scores of Fred   87

**The Marianne Frostig Developmental Test of Visual
Perception**   91

*Chapter 6. WHAT HAVE WE LEARNED FROM
RESEARCH?*   94

Selective Attention   96

What Is Selective Attention?   96

SELECTIVE ATTENTION AND LEARNING   97

SELECTIVE ATTENTION AND PERFORMANCE   100

Selective Attention and Learning Disabilities   101

Research on Selective Attention   101

SIGNAL DETECTION   102

DICHOTIC LISTENING   103

INCIDENTAL LEARNING   104

COMPONENT SELECTION   105

HEART RATE   107

What Does All of This Mean?   110

The Development of Selective Attention   111

OVEREXCLUSIVE ATTENTION   112

OVERINCLUSIVE ATTENTION   113

SELECTIVE ATTENTION   114

A DEVELOPMENTAL MODEL   115

*Implications for Working with the Learning-disabled
Child*   117

INCREASED DISTINCTIVENESS OF STIMULI   118

REWARDS FOR SELECTIVELY ATTENDING   120

TEACHING RESPONSE STRATEGIES   121

TARGETING TRAINING PROCEDURES   121

Chapter 7. WHAT CAN BE DONE FOR THE LEARNING–DISABLED CHILD?

Chapter 7. WHAT CAN BE DONE FOR THE
LEARNING–DISABLED CHILD?   124

Two Approaches   126

Focus Determines Action   127

Cognitive Methods of Intervention   128

Stop, Look, Listen, and Think!   128

"Here's How"   131

What Is Impulsiveness?   132

Behavioral Methods of Intervention   133

Behavior Is a Function of Its Consequences   133

"Put Not Your Trust in Vinegar—"   134

"—Molasses Catches Flies!"   134

Raymond   135

Behavior Abhors a Vacuum   136

How the Parent Can Help   137

Tokens and Prizes   139

"But Isn't That a Bribe?"   142

"Why Reward Doing One's Duty?"   143

"How Long Will This Go On?"   144

"And What about Her Brother?"   144

Chapter 8. WHAT ABOUT THE CHILD WHO
REFUSES TO GO TO SCHOOL?   145

School Refusal   145

Truancy   145

School Phobia 147

    How Does School Phobia Start? 147

    An Ounce of Prevention 148

    What to Do? 150

    A Paradox 151

    Early Intervention 155

    Other Forms of Managing School Phobias 157

Separation Anxiety 158

Lesson Refusal 159

Rewards 160

Punishment 161

Chapter 9. THE CHILD WHOSE BEHAVIOR IS A
SOURCE OF TROUBLE 163

The Aggressive Child 163

What Is Aggression? 164

Aggression Is a Response 165

Anger and Aggression 168

Aggression Can Be Learned 169

Aggression and Punishment 170

"Get It Out of Your System" 171

Can One Raise a Nonaggressive Child? 172

The Management of Classroom Problems 173

What One Can Learn in School 175

Who Are These Children? 176

What Teachers Notice 177

If You Must Scold, At Least Don't Shout! 181

SUMMING UP 186

Labels Can Be Deceptive 186

Tests Don't Always Tell 187

**Hyperactivity and Learning Disability Are Not
Synonymous** 188

Attention Has Many Facets 188

Learning-disabled Children Can Learn 189

Strategies for Teaching Strategies of Learning   189

Learning Not to Go to School   190

Fighting Aggression   190

ANNOTATED REFERENCES   192

INDEX   199

PREFACE

On Giving Psychology Away

In recent years we have witnessed a very encouraging development in psychological research: Psychologists have come out of
the laboratory and gone into the home, the school, and the
playground. While many continue to conduct important and
necessary research on those problems which can be studied
only in the laboratory, other psychologists are now examining
the complex problems of children and families which can be
studied only where children and families are to be found: in the
real world.

Because they are investigating questions about everyday
problems of everyday living, psychologists are beginning to be
in the position of suggesting answers to some of these questions. This development has, in turn, resulted in another wel-
come advance. No longer are answers to psychological questions the arcane knowledge of professional healers and
specialized helpers, but the methods for healing and helping
are increasingly being made available to people who used to be
thought of as the lay public. What is more, much of the healing
and helping has come out of the privacy of the professional's
consulting room and begun to take place where the problems
are: in the home and in the classroom where parents, and the
teachers, and the children themselves have become active part-
ners in the process of bringing about constructive psychological
change. It may be no exaggeration to view these developments
as nothing short of revolutionary.

Some years ago, in giving his Presidential address to the
American Psychological Association, Dr. George A. Miller

impressed on his colleagues that it was their task "to give psychology away." He correctly pointed out that there would never be enough of them to work directly on helping with the countless problems of human behavior for which psychologists are beginning to have some answers. The only way in which psychologists could be useful to humanity was for them to share their knowledge with other people so that they might learn to help themselves and each other.

It is in this spirit that I set about writing this book. With it I hope to tell parents and teachers and others who care about children some of the things I know regarding children with learning disabilities and children with school-related conduct problems. By sharing this knowledge, by thus giving psychology away, I may be able to suggest some ways in which the science of human behavior might be put to use by those who live and work with these troubled children.

I had previously written two textbooks about children with problems: *Psychological Disorders of Children* (1974) and *Psychological Aspects of Learning Disabilities and Reading Disorders* (1976). Though not particularly esoteric, they contain the kind of technical detail that is of interest only to a relatively limited group of readers. Both books, however, deal with problems which are of immediate concern to the many who raise and educate children. I thus saw a lot of merit in the suggestion of my esteemed friend, Professor Norman Garmezy, the editorial consultant to my publisher, that I prepare a book written especially for people who are neither psychologists nor training to become psychologists but who have use for what psychology has to offer.

Giving psychology away entails some risks. By writing for the general public, one enters an arena where books purporting to tell how to gain instant insight into oneself and others compete with manuals on how to achieve immediate social success, personal happiness, emotional wisdom, or contact with the mysteries of the universe. All of this is often hawked as psychology even though the writers may be members of the clergy, physicians, or former salespeople and engineers. As a university professor of psychology one is somewhat loath to have one's book on the same shelf with these facile recipes for better living. Wishing to share what I know without tarnishing my academic credentials, I have sought to hew as closely as possible to psychological facts that have been reasonably well established by the research of responsible investigators. I have avoided personal speculations and unsupported statements or recommendations. Thus, I hope that what I am giving away is indeed psychology and not a brand of psychological snake oil.

Besides the relatively minor risk to one's academic vanity, giving psychology away entails a larger, social risk. It is the risk that psychological knowledge about how to influence and change behavior might be used by those who would apply it to selfish or nefarious ends. I know of no certain protection against this risk. It would surely be futile to try guarding against this risk by having psychologists keep their knowledge to themselves. Knowledge is a tool and like all other tools, it can be used for good as well as for evil. Psychology is no exception. When we know how to change a child's behavior we can, like Fagin, train children to steal for us, or we can help them acquire more acceptable skills. Psychology may be able to tell us how to get to a goal; it cannot show us what that goal should be. That depends on our values and our priorities. Recognizing this, those who would use psychology should examine their values and make them public so that others, with different values, may have the opportunity to bring their opinions to bear.

My own values, as reflected in the pages which follow, are that education and knowledge are good; that it is desirable that children learn what the school has to offer; that going to school is therefore important; and that once in school it is well for children to attend to the teacher and bad to engage in behavior that hurts others or keeps them from learning. I suspect that most who read this will share these values, but we must recognize that they are no more than our opinions and that we should carefully listen to others who might disagree with us.

What Do We Have to Give Away?

There are those among my colleagues in psychology who would argue that since we still know so little and since what we know is still so tentative, it is premature and presumptuous to communicate our knowledge to the public. I recognize that much of the information we psychologists can now communicate comes from a limited number of studies, conducted under highly specific conditions, where the results are circumscribed by statistical probabilities which fall far short of absolute certainty. We often do not know whether these findings would hold true under different conditions and with different children, and it is not unusual that a later study contradicts or refutes the findings from earlier work. I am aware of the fact that our knowledge is tentative and likely to be revised by further research, but I also know that children and their parents and teachers can't wait until the slow and painstaking process of scientific investigation has arrived at irrefutable certainty. In fact, such certainty may be unattainable.

There is no point pretending that today's psychology has all the answers to questions about children's learning and children's behavior. Indeed, it would be dishonest to claim that psychology has many of these answers. We have made a beginning in understanding the conditions under which learning takes place, and we know some of the circumstances that can interfere with learning. We believe we have established the general principles by which learning can be improved and behavior changed, but if one made a list of all the questions that might be asked about problems which can trouble children in school, there would no doubt be more questions that still remain unanswered than those where answers can be given without hesitation or qualification. Anyone who makes claims to the contrary should be suspected of deceit.

Reading a book such as this calls for an ability to tolerate the ambiguity which today's state of psychology presents, but I am sure that sharing our uncertainty and admitting our ignorance is more constructive than either trying to hide what we do know or painting a rosy but dishonest picture which, though reassuring to read, is bound to lead to early disappointment.

How Should We Give It Away?

The subject matter of psychology is so complex that it can be approached from several, probably equally valid, directions and perspectives. There are those who prefer to examine human behavior in terms of motivations and emotions; others choose to focus on the processes of thought and memory. There are psychologists who insist that only phenomena that can be observed are legitimate objects of scientific study, while others view this approach as artifically limiting their inquiry. Some psychologists like to study events in small, isolated units, while others attempt to examine more global aspects of behavior. Many investigators believe that they must employ the methods of natural science if they are to progress in their study of psychology, while other scholars aver that the essence of human existence must be explored through different means.

It would be possible to write a comprehensive book about the topic of this volume in which most or all of these orientations and approaches could be represented. I suspect, however, that such a survey would be more likely to confuse than to inform and so I have decided to limit my presentation to the orientation which I find most congenial in my own work. I believe that this admittedly biased approach will not only give the reader a clearer picture but that it will also permit me to advance an authentic version of the material since I present what I know from my own point of view.

What is my point of view? It is that psychology is indeed a natural science and that its subject matter, human behavior, can only be studied by objective means. I believe that the major focus of psychology should be on those phenomena which can be observed or made observable and that speculative inferences about so-called inner processes must be drawn with great circumspection. That is not to say I don't believe that people think. It would be folly to assert that. But I do believe that one can study thinking only indirectly by observing the consequences of thoughts as they are reflected in what people do or say.

Two other convictions of mine should be made explicit. One is that all behavior, whether adaptive or maladaptive, normal or abnormal, follows the same principles. Thus, the principles we can observe operating in the life of the well-functioning person must also be assumed to guide the disordered behavior of people in trouble. Related to this is a second conviction: Human development is a continuous process and children with problems are on the same continuum with children who are doing well. Troubled children may be moving on the developmental track more slowly than others and some may even be standing still on that track, but they are on the same track nonetheless. Another way of saying this is that we are not dealing with deficiencies or abnormalities but with developmental disabilities and individual differences.

I believe that this approach to psychology is essentially positive and optimistic. I think psychology can and must help people and that the ultimate goal of our endeavors is to help all children develop their fullest potential as effective and constructive human beings. What kind of psychologist am I? Call me a behavioral humanist.

ALAN O. ROSS

A Note on Confidentiality

Names are always fictitious in the various illustrative case examples used in this book. All identifying characteristics have been changed in order to assure the confidentiality of clinical relationships. Even the people on whom the illustrations are based could not possibly recognize themselves, and any apparent similarity is pure coincidence. The one exception to this is the case of Judy, my daughter, who really did perfect her bicycle-riding in her sleep.

LEARNING DISABILITY

Chapter 1

A LEARNING–DISABLED CHILD

What Is the Matter with Fred?

Fred is nine years old. He is repeating second grade but his reading level is that of a child in first grade. He has trouble blending sounds, mistakes *b* for *d* and vice versa, sometimes reads words backward so that "pot" becomes "top," and even when he succeeds in his painstaking way to read a sentence, he fails to understand its meaning. While his writing is laborious and full of spelling errors, Fred has no difficulty with arithmetic and does especially well when problems are presented to him orally and not in writing.

Fred's father is a successful corporation lawyer who had gone to an Ivy League college and earned his law degree from a highly prestigious law school. Fred's mother holds a master's degree in modern languages and teaches French at an expensive private school. Their boy's trouble in school is a source of consternation and disappointment to them, especially since their two older children, a girl and a boy, breezed through elementary school and are doing outstanding work in junior high and high school, respectively.

There was no hint of Fred's school problem in his early childhood. He seemed alert, walked early, learned stair-climbing and tricycle-riding with ease, and talked in sentences no later than his older siblings. When his kindergarten class was examined for reading readiness, Fred's performance was a bit uneven and there was a brief moment when the school considered delaying his entry into first grade because of what they called his immaturity, but his teacher and parents soon agreed that a child as bright as Freddy should be able to manage.

But Freddy did not manage. Maybe he was not as bright as everyone thought. After six months in first grade his teacher suggested that he be given an intelligence test. His parents knew that the IQs of their older children were around 130 and they had long been curious as to whether Fred was also that bright. A psychologist whom they consulted privately gave Fred an intelligence test. While the results were a bit puzzling since Fred did well on some parts of the test and poorly on others, his overall score was well above average. The psychologist was reluctant to give Freddy's parents his IQ score, but after repeated questioning, she mentioned the figure 105, adding that Freddy should not be having any trouble with first-grade work. Maybe, suggested the psychologist, Freddy was emotionally disturbed; the drawings the boy had done for her seemed rather immature.

The next series of tests were therefore directed at Freddy's emotional state. Their results suggested that Fred seemed somewhat unsure of himself, a bit too dependent for his age, somewhat troubled by his aggressive feelings, and a bit on the impulsive side. None of this was serious, however, and it failed to explain why the boy should be having trouble learning to read. Did the parents ever have Fred's eyes examined? Maybe he had trouble with vision.

This led to a thorough eye examination by an ophthalmologist who found some mild astigmatism in the boy's left eye, not serious enough to explain the reading problem but calling for correction nevertheless. Freddy was thus fitted with eyeglasses which he hates to wear and about which he and his parents continue to have frequent quarrels. In the course of obtaining the first of many sets of glasses from the local optician, the mother mentioned Fred's reading problem while the frame was being fitted and the optician said something about an optometrist who gave perceptual training to children with visual-motor problems. Fred's parents called the ophthalmologist who had seen the child and asked whether such training might help him too. The eye doctor told them that she knew nothing about that program and could not advise them one way or another.

As their confusion increased, Fred's parents were called to his school, where the teacher complained that the boy was not making any progress at all in his reading. In addition, they were told he was beginning to get into fights with other children and that he had trouble remaining in his seat. "He almost seems as if he were hyperactive," said the teacher. "Maybe you should have him checked for brain damage."

That bit of news came as quite a shock to Fred's family. His mother did have rather prolonged labor when he was born and once, when he was around eighteen months old, he had fallen out of a supermarket shopping cart and hit his head on the floor. If he were brain damaged, it would explain his school problem, but the prospects for a child with a damaged brain were very upsetting to contemplate. Through a referral from their family physician they next found themselves in the office of a neurologist. Fred was given a neurological examination, including a test of the electrical impulses in his brain—an electroencephalogram or EEG, for short—but the results were inconclusive. "There are no signs of brain damage," said the neurologist, much to the relief of the parents, "but we may be dealing with a case of minimal cerebral dysfunction syndrome." Being a lawyer, Fred's father wanted to know what the evidence was for this verdict. There was little direct evidence, said the neurologist, but he reminded the parents of the boy's otherwise unexplained difficulties in school. At any rate, he recommended a trial prescription of a medication Fred was to take three times a day.

Thus began the period of the green pills. Fred's mother was to give him one in the morning before breakfast, one in the afternoon when he came home, and at noon he was to go to the school nurse who was to give him his midday dose before lunch. Before long, getting Freddy to take his pills became another source of arguments and conflict. Fred resented the trip to the nurse. First the glasses; now this. The other kids were making fun of him and he hated school "anyhow." The mother noticed that Fred did not have his usual appetite, that his playing seemed less vigorous, and that he just did not seem her old Freddy. A check with the school revealed that Fred no longer got into trouble about his sitting still and fighting. His reading? It was as poor as ever. They could not possibly promote him to third grade. Had the parents thought of taking him out and sending him to a private school specializing in work with mildly retarded and brain-damaged children? But Freddy is neither retarded nor brain damaged. He is not emotionally disturbed and his eyesight is fine. He comes from a home that values learning and rewards achievement in school. What is the matter with Fred?

The Problem and Its Labels

In every classroom in the land there sits at least one child like Fred, a child who is obviously and demonstrably bright but who fails to keep up with his class in one or more subject matters. These children differ from one another in many ways. Some are restless and move about a lot, some fight with other children, some flit from one interest to the next, never staying with any one task for very long, some are easily distracted from what they are doing, and some have trouble paying attention. As is true of children in general, no two of these children are ever alike. They have just one thing in common: they show a discrepancy between the school performance expected of them on the basis of their potential and the performance they actually produce. We have come to refer to them as *learning disabled.*

Like the child we called Freddy, such children are a source of consternation, irritation, and despair to teachers and parents alike, and the reactions of these adults inevitably increases the pressure on the child who is already frustrated and distressed. It is, therefore, not surprising that such children develop a dislike for school, anger at teachers, jealousy toward successful siblings and peers, negative self-evaluations, and behavior, such as aggression, which further complicates their lives and the task of finding out what is wrong with them. Thus, it is not unusual for cause and effect to be confused so that people will blame the learning problem on, say, the aggression instead of recognizing that the aggression is the result of the learning problem.

From Dunce to Dyslexia. We can assume that such children have existed ever since the introduction of formal education. In the past they probably used to leave school at an early age until laws calling for universal education made continued school attendance mandatory. We can also assume that over the years these children have met various fates, depending on the contemporary wisdom by which responsible adults sought to explain why a child fails to learn. It is thus likely that these children have been dismissed as dumb, lazy, or as lacking the will to learn. Many, no doubt, have stood in corners wearing a dunce cap, while countless others have been ridiculed, castigated, made to stay after class, or ordered to engage in punitive, repetitive exercises like writing one hundred times, "I must pay attention." Adults are often very inventive when it comes to thinking up ways to punish a child. Inevitably, the basis of these actions has been the assumption that there is something wrong with the child and that somehow or other one must try to straighten out the child. This is not too far removed from the primitive idea that the child is possessed by a demon who must be cast out. It was always the child who was to blame, never the teacher or the teaching method. The various labels that have been used over the years to identify these children reflect this notion.

From dunce and dullard and dolt, we gradually developed more sophisticated sounding terms, some with graeco-latin pretensions. Underachievement, perceptual-motor disorder, psycholinguistic retardation, perceptual handicap, hyperactivity, hyperkinesis, hypermotility, distractibility, impulsivity, dyslexia, dyscalculia, brain injury, minimal brain damage, minimal cerebral dysfunction, and psychoneurological learning disability have all had their day or still have currency. At the present time, the favored term is learning disability or specific learning disability. Note that all of these terms are nouns so that they are used to complete such sentences as, "This child has . . ." or "This child suffers from. . . ." We no longer speak of demons which must be cast out. We speak instead of disease-like entities which must be cured. An educational problem has thus been cast in the terms of a medical problem, neatly shifting the responsibility from the teacher to the physician.

We are dealing with children who fail to benefit from regular classroom instruction in one or more areas of academic subject matter despite at least average intelligence and in the

absence of demonstrable physical, emotional, or cultural handicaps. That sentence describes the problem. Provided we mean
no more than that by the term, we can say that these are
learning-disabled children, but we should not fall into the trap
of saying that these children "have" a learning disability, the
way we would say that other children have asthma.

Why? When people encounter a puzzling phenomenon,
such as an intelligent child who has inordinate trouble learning
to read, they quite naturally ask why this is the case. They wish
to understand the cause of the problem, to explain how this
state of affairs came about. The trouble is that "why" questions,
when asked about phenomena of nature, are likely to lead to
deceptive answers. Causes are often invented and explanations
may be sought in circular labels.

Humanity, throughout its history, has asked, "Why?" and
settled (for a time) for explanatory fictions. Take for example the
fact that the position of the sun changes from the horizon to the
zenith in the course of a morning. An observer, inferring that
the sun is rising, asks, "Why does the sun rise?" The spurious
answers to this question have ranged from anthropomorphisms
about the sun-god Helios driving his fiery wagon across the sky
to teleologic speculations about life's need for daylight.

No less fallacious than these answers to the "why" question are explanatory labels which merely restate the observation
but explain nothing. "Why does the flower grow in the direction of the sun?" can be answered with, "Because it is heliotropic," but this is no more than a Greek way of saying that the
flower grows in the direction of the sun. Nothing has been
explained although a naïve questioner may well be satisfied that
an answer has been supplied.

These fallacies have their counterpart in the realm of learning-disabled children. A child who has trouble learning
prompts one to ask "why?" which may elicit the answer,
"Because he has minimal brain damage." This, as we shall see
later, is the sun-god Helios in a new disguise. Analogous to the
explanatory label *heliotropic* is the term *dyslexia*. Here the
question is, "Why does this child have difficulty learning to
read?" The answer is, "Because he has dyslexia." What has
happened? Reading difficulty has been translated into Greek,

and inaccurately at that, for the literal meaning of *dyslexia* is "word-sickness." Nothing has been explained, though there must be hundreds of teachers and thousands of parents whose puzzlement about a child who cannot read has been assauaged because they think that they now know the reason for the problem.

What? If questions phrased in terms of "why" lead to such unsatisfactory explanations, what questions should one ask? What is it really that a parent of a learning-disabled child wants to know? Not *why* the child is the way he or she is (that is essentially no more than idle curiosity) but *what* the parent can do for the child so that the problem can be solved. The explanation we must seek lies not in the answer to "why?" but in the answer to "what?" What are the circumstances under which this child's difficulty is manifested? What alterations in these circumstances reduce the difficulty? What can I do to help my child? Answers to these questions do far more than satisfy idle curiosity; they do something constructive for the child even though the original cause of the problem may remain unknown and the "why" question unsatisfied.

Labels and Their Consequences. When a problem is given a label, the problem is not explained; the question of why the problem arose is not answered. Not only that, but labels have a way of guiding the behavior of those who use or hear the label. If a child who refuses to go to school is labeled *truant,* one series of events is set in motion; if he is labeled *school phobic,* an entirely different sequence of steps will ensue. The same is true in the case of the child whose school achievement fails to live up to our expectations. It makes a lot of difference in terms of what happens to the child whether he or she is labeled *mentally retarded* or *emotionally disturbed,* a lot of difference whether the designation is *brain damaged* or *culturally disadvantaged.* Yet labels such as these are often loosely bandied about and almost casually attached to given children, not because the child will thus be helped but because the label absolves somebody of responsibility for doing something for the child by transferring this responsibility to another school, department, or discipline.

We shall presently turn to a detailed examination of the

various labels which have been used and how they tend to determine what people do with and for the child, but first we must seek to spell out just what kind of children we have in mind when we talk about learning-disabled children.

Who Is a Learning-disabled Child?

There are many children who don't do well in school, many children who have difficulty in learning, but not all are learning disabled. Who are the ones who are not?

The Learning-disabled Child Is Not Mentally Retarded. A child whose intellectual capacity is below the normal range will have difficulty in deriving benefit from unspecialized school instruction. His or her difficulty almost always affects every area of behavior which involves learning. Such a child will have been late in the acquisition of language, slow in learning such motor skills as stair-climbing, and slow in learning such self-help skills as feeding and dressing. In school, such a child will have trouble in all subject areas, be it writing, spelling, reading, or arithmetic.

There are many labels which are used to identify such children. The most familiar are mental retardation, mental deficiency, and mental subnormality. One differentiates various levels of severity, ranging from mild to profound, and there are at least two major groups, those whose problem is due to a known neurological or biochemical defect, and those whose subnormality is a reflection of the fact that in the human population some are very bright and some are very dull. This latter group, sometimes referred to as *familial defectives,* will have many close relatives who are also of subnormal intelligence. This is another characteristic which permits one to differentiate between the mentally subnormal and the learning disabled.

The Learning-disabled Child Is Not Physically Impaired. A child with a physical impairment, such as poor eyesight or difficulty in hearing, will have difficulty learning in a classroom where no effort is made to take this handicap into account. Again, one should not speak of such a child as learning disabled if that category is to be at all meaningful. When an apparently bright child encounters difficulties with school-related learning, it stands to reason that one should make certain that the child has the physical capacity to benefit from the school experience. An eye examination is usually one of the first steps recommended, because if the child can't see what is written on the chalkboard learning would obviously be difficult for him. There will also be learning-disabled children who are nearsighted, or otherwise in need of corrective lenses, but their visual problem is not the basis of their difficulty. Neither are other physical problems, some more subtle or more obvious than poor eyesight. Thus, learning-disabled children are not children with cerebral palsy or children with metabolic defects. They are not children with gross neurological disorders, nor, as we shall have occasion to explain, are they children with brain damage. In some school systems, learning-disabled children are placed in special classes for the physically handicapped. This is usually an administrative convenience. If this results in highly individualized teaching for such children, it may be better than having them remain in a regular classroom where no allowances are made for their problem. But one must not lose sight of the fact that the learning-disabled child is not a child with a physical impairment, and so does not really belong in a class for such children.

The Learning-disabled Child Is Not Emotionally Disturbed. While emotional problems are not the cause of such children's difficulty with learning, they may well be the effect. If a child sits in class and, despite his best efforts, is unable to learn and people blame him and reprimand him and punish him for not learning; when his parents show their concern and increasing irritation or anxiety; when he is taken from one expert to another in order to find out what is "wrong" with him; when younger brothers or sisters succeed where he is failing, one should not be surprised if such a child were to develop a negative attitude toward himself or school or studying; if he were to become jealous of successful siblings and peers and express this in aggressive outbursts; or if he showed signs of tension and anxiety, unhappiness or withdrawal.

After a while it may be difficult to sort out what is cause and what is effect, for the child's emotional state may well add further complications to his school performance. By the time some of these children come to the attention of professional experts it is easy to confuse cause and effect. Hence, it is not at all unusual for learning-disabled children to be identified as emotionally disturbed and to receive treatment that is focused on their anxiety, their aggression, or their depression. While these secondary emotional reactions are sometimes alleviated, their problem with learning does not go away because it is the cause and not the result of the emotional problems. It is not enough to make a child feel better about being a failure in school, not enough to get his parents to reduce their pressures or their punitive reactions; what is needed is help with the learning problem and no form of psychotherapy alone can accomplish that. Furthermore, just as a learning-disabled child does not belong in a special class for the mentally retarded or the physically handicapped, so does he not belong in a special class for the emotionally disturbed.

The Learning-disabled Child Is Not Culturally Disadvantaged. This statement calls for an immediate clarification. Just as a learning-disabled child may also have poor eyesight, so may a learning-disabled child also come from a cultural background that places him or her at a disadvantage in a school which fails to recognize cultural diversity. Some culturally disadvantaged children may be learning disabled; some learning-disabled children may be culturally disadvantaged. The point to stress is that it is a mistake to include under the rubric learning disabled those children who have difficulty benefiting from school instruction because their cultural or language background differs from the mythical average child for whom the instruction and its underlying expectations are geared. It is a disservice to both the learning disabled and the child with a minority background to indiscriminately classify both as belonging to the same group of children with special educational needs. One would think that this is so obvious as not to require mentioning. But walk into any class for learning-disabled children in any one of our larger cities and you will find children who are unable to meet the academic goals of the regular classroom and who come from homes where the parents speak a dialect or a foreign language or where school attendance and school achievement are very low on the scale of values. What is more, you will find children whose disruptive behavior or deviant manners made them unacceptable to the teachers in the regular class, who managed to relieve themselves of these children by attaching to them the label learning disabled. As we shall see when we turn to a discussion of hyperactivity and the use of medications, it is not unusual to find such children being "controlled" by irresponsibly prescribed drugs.

Who Is a Learning-disabled Child? We thus return to the question with which we started. If learning-disabled children are not mentally retarded, not physically handicapped, not emotionally disturbed, and not culturally or educationally disadvantaged, who are they? All existing definitions focus on what the learning-disabled child is not. What he is will occupy most of this book. But, anticipating much of what will come later, we can define a learning-disabled child as:

> a child of at least average intelligence whose academic performance is impaired by a developmental lag in the ability to sustain selective attention. Such a child requires specialized instruction in order to permit the use of his or her full intellectual potential.

A learning-disabled child is neither damaged nor permanently impaired. The disability is an inability to make use of the unspecialized instruction usually found in the typical classroom. Given proper and specialized instruction, the disability disappears. The problem is thus an educational problem, not a psychological problem or a medical problem. The responsibility for helping these children ultimately rests with the educators, for a learning disability is not so much a lack in the child's ability to learn as it is a lack in the educator's ability to identify and teach children with special educational needs.

This is not an attack on teachers, for it is not a matter of assigning blame but of pointing out that all too little is known about learning-disabled children and that the little that we do know has not been adequately disseminated. The "state of the art" is, unfortunately, rather dismal. We don't know how to identify the learning-disabled child *before* he or she falls behind in class and feels like a misfit, and even at that point it often takes us far too long to assess the problem correctly. Once we do, we find ourselves in the position of trying various methods in a hit-or-miss fashion. In sincere efforts to help, we follow various educational fads whose effectiveness is unproven or we apply techniques that are based on no more than the pronouncements of often self-appointed authorities. The individual teacher cannot be blamed for this state of affairs—but neither can the child!

What about Brain Damage?

It is not too difficult for people to accept the statement that learning-disabled children are neither mentally or physically defective, nor emotionally, culturally, or educationally handicapped. The reason is that these impairments would be relatively easy to see or ascertain, particularly for a parent of one of these children. But what about brain damage? The brain, hidden as it is from view and, unlike the heart, functioning in silence, is easily the most important and, at the same time, the least understood part of the human body. There is a mysterious, almost miraculous quality about the brain. Most of us think that we know what it does; yet we have little or no idea of how it goes about its functions. It is intriguing to realize that when we think about brain functions we must use that very brain to do the thinking. Thinking about thinking, as it were. Some have even suggested that the reason science has made so little progress in understanding the functioning of the brain lies in the fact that there is a logical limit to how far the human brain can go in studying itself!

Since we know so relatively little about the brain, it is all too easy to attribute all manner of functions—and malfunctions—to that mysterious part of our body. One can say with a great deal of assurance that learning involves the brain and that learning takes place in the brain. Can one say with equal assurance that if learning fails to take place, something must be wrong in the brain? The answer to this depends on what one means by "something wrong." Obviously, if the brain is involved in learning and learning does not occur, the brain must, in some fashion, not be functioning as we expect it to. But does that mean that something is "wrong"? Things can be wrong with the brain in a variety of ways. Parts of the brain may have failed to develop; parts may have been damaged before, during, or shortly after the child's birth; illness or injury may have left a lesion which disrupts the working of the brain. All of these are ways in which there could be something wrong with the brain, but none of these are the case with learning-disabled children. Nobody has ever demonstrated that learning-disabled children are brain damaged though many have claimed that this is the reason for their problem.

Because learning is a function of the brain and since this function is impaired in the case of the learning-disabled child, some have come to speak of brain dysfunction in place of brain damage. What do we mean when we use the word *function?* One meaning of function is the normal and special action of an organ. In that sense, we can say that learning is a function of the brain, just as we say that digestion is a function of the gastro-intestinal system. The other meaning of the word function has to do with the relationship between two events which are dependent upon and vary with each other. We are familiar with that notion from mathematics where one says that x is a function of y. When the value of x changes, the value of y also changes. (When the value of the dollar goes down, the value of the dime also declines.) These two meanings of the word function, the physiological and the mathematical meaning, are often confounded when people speak of brain functions. They say, "Learning is a function of the brain," meaning that learning is something the brain does, but at the same time they expect some sort of fixed relationship between learning and brain activity, as if the two were known to vary with each other in some mathematical fashion—as if less learning meant less brain, or defective learning, defective brain.

Observing a problem in learning and attributing this to a brain dysfunction, many assume that this means that there is a physical abnormality, a damage or lesion in the child's brain. From this it is all too easy to conclude that children who have difficulty learning are brain damaged, thus introducing unwarranted notions of traumatic causes, irreversibility, limited potential, and need for medical care. There is, as we have said and shall endeavor to support, no evidence for the assumption that learning-disabled children have structural abnormalities in their brain. Nothing is "wrong" with their brain in that sense. This fact was slowly recognized by those who look for brain damage behind almost every human frailty, from alcoholism to zoophilia, so that brain damage came to be modified by the word *minimal.*

Minimal brain damage is a way of saying "even though we can't demonstrate the damage, we know it is there, only minimally." Eventually, the word *damage,* even with the modifier, could no longer be defended and the term *minimal brain dysfunction* was thus introduced and given currency. Ultimately, even that had to be disguised and the last defenders of this point of view now speak of MBD; it is the fading smile of the Cheshire cat once known as brain damage.

We shall have more to say about brain functions in a later chapter, but first it may be well to take a look at the history of this problem in order to see how we got into all this confusion.

Chapter 2

HOW DID IT ALL START?

A Bit of History

Our tale begins in Frankfurt am Main shortly after World War I when Kurt Goldstein studied the aftereffects of brain injuries sustained by German soldiers. He was interested in finding out about the functions of the various parts of the brain and particularly of the frontal lobes. When a scientist wishes to investigate the functions of specific parts of a whole that works in unison, the best method is to remove or disconnect one part at a time and to observe the effect of such interventions on the working of the total organ. In studying the functions of the human brain, it is obviously impossible to conduct experiments that involve the removal or disconnecting of selected parts of the brain simply for the sake of research.

Investigators of brain functions can't purposely cut out parts of the human brain. They must thus rely on so-called experiments of nature or, in this case, on such unnatural events as wars, tumors, or accidents which, having caused damage to the brain, call for surgical intervention. By studying the effect of such surgery on the behavior of the patient, an investigator can draw conclusions about the function of the portion of the brain that has been damaged or removed. These conclusions are wrought with pitfalls, however. The person being studied has not simply had a specific part of the brain removed. He has also experienced the trauma that led to the surgery, may have sustained damage to other parts of his body, and has spent weeks or months in the hospital, recovering from all of this.

Furthermore, brain injuries due to accidents, bullets, shrapnel, or even tumors are usually quite extensive and anything but neatly circumscribed so that one usually can't say exactly what part of the brain was removed. Any statement one might make about the relationship between brain and behavior is thus necessarily vague and grossly speculative. Take a soldier who has been hit on the left side of the skull by a piece of shrapnel that penetrated his brain. After a neurosurgeon has removed the bone splinters, the piece of jagged metal, and cleaned up the area in the best way possible and after the soldier has sufficiently recovered so he can be studied, one finds that he can no longer write his name. What can one conclude? That this ability is a function of a specific one cubic inch of brain? Hardly.

AFTEREFFECTS OF BRAIN INJURY IN WAR

During the 1915 battle in the Argonne Forest, a shell fragment had penetrated his skull and become lodged in the left side of his brain. The piece of shrapnel had been removed during surgery. There had been some mild paralysis of the right arm shortly after the injury, but no particularly conspicuous disturbance of speech had been observed. When Bruno B. was examined two years later, he complained of occasional headaches and dizziness, but except for a slight impairment in the movements of his right arm, no physical symptoms could be observed. During more detailed psychological study, however, several other problems were readily apparent.

Herr B. was able to say how many objects, such as blocks, had been placed before him, but he could not respond to the request to count, that is, to say the numbers, starting with one. He could do this only when the examiner started the series for him. Then he was able to complete it. Yet, if he were interrupted, he could not continue but had to start over again. He also had difficulty stopping at an arbitrary point upon demand and would try to continue counting until he was decisively stopped. He would be at a loss in a conversation if the topic shifted, although he was able to participate in discussions of a familiar topic or about the immediate situation. Shifting from one thought process to another always gave him trouble. Thus, he would be able to read a word at a time and to spell it at another time, but when he was asked to read the word and then immediately spell it, he could not do it.

Another area of difficulty for Bruno B. was thinking about things that were not immediately present. For example, he would fail on performances which had meaning only in relation to the future. Asked to set his watch to the time at which he would be having supper, he behaved as if he had no idea of what was expected of him. Yet, at supper time, he could look at his watch and give the correct time. Similarly, while he was able to find his way around the rather complicated hospital building, he was quite unable to describe the relations of one room to another or to say which floor was on top of the one where he was presently located.

Based on descriptions in K. Goldstein, *Aftereffects of brain-injuries in war.* New York: Grune & Stratton, 1942.

Brain-injured Soldiers. Goldstein's study of the severely impaired individuals on his hospital service led him to the conclusion that brain damage results in forced responsiveness to stimuli, difficulty in differentiating between a figure and its background, and an inability to deal with abstract concepts.

Forced responsiveness to stimuli can be demonstrated when one gives a brain-injured person a set of disks differing in shape and in color with the instructions to sort these into groups on the basis of some similarity. Some people will sort according to color, some according to shape. When one then mixes the disks up again and asks that they be sorted on a different basis, the normal person with unimpaired brain functions will readily shift to the alternate sorting principle; having previously sorted by color, he will now sort by shape or vice versa. Goldstein's brain-damaged soldiers were unable to do this. They remained *stimulus bound*—captured, as it were, by either the color or the shape aspect of the disks and unable to let go, unable to shift and thus to disregard incidental, unessential aspects of a stimulus.

Difficulty in differentiating between figure and background would manifest itself in a person's inability to reproduce a simple rhythm. A rhythm is a pattern of sounds, interspersed by silence (pauses) where the sounds represent figure and the pauses the background. Analogous demonstrations can be found in the visual realm where a line of dots

. .   . .

is seen as a pattern (in pairs of two) because we recognize the difference between figure and background. Goldstein was able to show that brain-injured patients experienced difficulties in dealing with these and related perceptual tasks. Many of these he adapted from the Gestalt school of psychology, which was becoming prominent at that time.

We should here point out that a statement about difficulty in distinguishing between figure and background is an inference because the internal operation necessary to reproduce a rhythm, for example, cannot be directly observed. We present a rhythm, ask a person to reproduce it, and find that he is unable to do so. Saying this is because he is unable to tell the sounds and pauses apart remains our guess, for it could be that he did not attend properly when the initial stimulus was presented, that he can't hold it in memory long enough to make the reproduction, or that he simply does not care to play our simple-minded game. We shall meet this dilemma again when we discuss the problems surrounding the study of learning.

Goldstein's studies are probably best remembered as having demonstrated the difficulty some brain-injured persons have with abstract concepts. He pointed out that such people can deal with concrete experiences but that they have trouble adopting, what he called, the *abstract attitude.* An example: Give a brain-injured individual a glass of water and ask him to demonstrate how he drinks. He will readily bring the glass to his lips and take a sip. Now give him an empty glass and ask him to show you how he *would* drink water out of it. Even a child could readily simulate the water-drinking act; Goldstein reports that his patients were unable to do so. They would be puzzled by the request. The "as if" approach required for this performance seemed no longer a part of their repertoire.

Other demonstrations of the concrete-abstract dimension can be found in tasks requiring the sorting of objects. Given a large array of various common articles, the severely brain-damaged individual may be able to sort them on the basis of their use (what you do with them) but not on the basis of such supraordinate categories as fruit, meats, and vegetables. To him the latter are all in one category—"you eat them." Difficulties in dealing with abstractions also manifested themselves in Goldstein's patients in that they were able to solve arithmetic problems only when numbers were represented by objects that could be handled.

In addition to these observations, Goldstein reported that his patients would have "catastrophic reactions" when they encountered situations with which they were unable to cope. These reactions are characterized by extreme disorganization of behavior, rage, despair, and disorientation. As if to ward off these reactions, the brain-injured individual reportedly sought a great deal of structure and order in his environment, invariance of stimulation, and repeated familiar actions over and over again.

Goldstein thus presented a picture of the severely brain-damaged adult as one who is stimulus bound, unable to deal with abstractions, incapable of differentiating between figure and ground, prone to catastrophic reactions, perseverative, meticulous, and orderly. By the standards of today's research, Goldstein's clinical observations and test procedures were primitive and imprecise. He used no controls to guard against his own biases, and from a few extremely brain-damaged and impaired individuals, he generalized to the functions of the normal brain. Nonetheless, his was a landmark contribution that influenced the thinking of many of his students and others who learned of his work. Among these were the psychiatrist Alfred A. Strauss and the developmental psychologist Heinz Werner.

Mentally Retarded Children. Our scene now shifts from the aftermath of World War I to the historical events surrounding World War II when Strauss and Werner, having been forced to leave Hitler's Germany, found themselves working together in the research department of the Wayne County Training School, an institution for the mentally retarded in Michigan. Strauss had published a paper in 1933, based on work he had done while still in Germany, in which he discussed the causes of profound mental deficiency. In it he suggested that brain damage was one important cause of retardation, and he and Werner pursued this idea in their work in Michigan.

When a person does not have an obvious history of an injury to the brain (as had been the case with Goldstein's war casualties), the determination of whether his brain is damaged must be based on indirect signs. One source of these is the person's behavior, and it is here that Goldstein's contributions came to find application in the work of Strauss and Werner. Seeking to differentiate between retarded children whose problem was due to brain injury and retarded children whose difficulty was related to familial factors, these investigators reasoned that children who manifest the disordered behavior found in Goldstein's brain-injured adults would have to be children whose brain had been damaged, thereby causing their retardation. Thus, they set out to look for figure-ground problems, difficulties in abstracting, stimulus-bound behavior, and perseveration among the retarded children at the Training School.

Because the work of Strauss and Werner was to have a major influence on those who later came to think about children with learning disabilities, it is well to point to the logical flaw in their reasoning. Adults who are presumed to have been normal prior to their brain injury seem to have trouble with figure-ground perception. It does not necessarily follow from this that retarded children who have trouble with figure-ground perception owe their retardation to brain damage. In the absence of an independent indication of brain damage it is fallacious to identify a child as brain injured merely on the basis of the observation that his behavior on a psychological test is similar to behavior manifested by brain-injured adults. A previously intact adult brain that has been damaged is very likely to function differently from the developing brain of a child. Even if the child's brain has sustained some damage, it is quite unlike that inflicted by the devastation wrought by a piece of shrapnel. That neither the adult war casualty nor the mentally retarded child can tell us very much about a normal child who is learning disabled would nowadays appear obvious.

The Perceptual Motorists

In their efforts to identify brain-injured children among the mentally retarded, Strauss and his coworkers employed various tasks on which the children they presumed to be brain damaged displayed performance difficulties. One of these tasks was a marble board on which the child was to reproduce a design presented by the examiner. A design composed of colored marbles is, of course, a figure; the spaces between the marbles and the surrounding board furnish the background. If a person has difficulty placing the marbles into the recesses on the board in such a way as to reproduce the design shown to him, the difficulty can be construed as reflecting the kind of figure-ground disorder Goldstein reported in his studies of brain-injured adults. It was this analogy between the performance difficulties of Goldstein's patients and the problems displayed by their mentally retarded children that led Strauss and Werner to the conclusion that the children were brain damaged.

The concept of figure-ground confusion has theoretical implications. These derive from the Gestalt school of psychology which flourished in Germany shortly before the Second World War. This approach to psychology did not win very many adherents in the United States, despite the fact that its most prominent proponents had emigrated to this country. This may have been the reason why references to figure-ground disturbances eventually disappeared from the writings of Strauss and his students, to be replaced by the term *perceptual-motor difficulties,* a term which implies fewer inferences about internal processes. It simply states that the person experiences difficulty when he perceives a stimulus by hearing, sight, or touch and is then asked to reproduce that stimulus by means of a motor movement.

Though perception is, technically speaking, also an internal process since it entails making some sense of the nerve impulse received by the sense organ, the idea of perceptual-motor behavior is more compatible with the tendency of American psychologists of that time to work, as far as possible, with terms which could be objectively defined, such as stimulus and response. At any rate, it soon became fashionable to speak of perceptual-motor disturbances and to view these as characteristic of children with brain damage.

When Strauss (together with Lehtinen) wrote about brain-injured children in 1947 in the influential *Psychopathology and Education of the Brain-injured Child,* he left no doubt about the definition of brain injury. "A brain-injured child," he wrote, "is a child who before, during, or after birth has received an injury to or suffered an infection of the brain." He pointed out that such a child may show disturbances in perception which prevent or impede a normal learning process so that special educational methods are needed. It is a shame that this straightforward statement was turned on its head by later writers. For while Strauss spoke of injury to the brain resulting in perceptual (and other) problems, perceptual problems have since come to be viewed as indications of brain injury in children for whom no injury to or infection of the brain has ever been demonstrated. Rain leaves puddles on the street, but a puddle on the street does not permit one to conclude that it has rained! Obviously, performance on a task such as the marble board can be interfered with by all kinds of problems other than those caused by damage to the brain.

From his studies of the mentally retarded, Strauss, together with his collaborators Kephart and Lehtinen, drew a series of conclusions regarding the education of brain-injured children. Among these was the recommendation that one reduce the number of distracting stimuli in the child's classroom environment. This was based on the assumption that such children have trouble focusing on the essential aspects of a learning situation and represents another version of the idea of figure-ground confusion. This recommendation eventually led to placing presumably distractible children into specially constructed cubicles which were supposed to limit the number of distractions.

A second recommendation dealt with giving brain-injured children perceptual-motor exercises. This was done on the questionable logic that if brain damage interferes with relating perceptual events and motor responses, the training of perceptual-motor coordination should somehow benefit the child. What this is supposed to do for the brain was never clearly stated. Speculations about the brain become, in fact, quite superfluous. If one observes perceptual-motor problems and considers these of importance, then improving perceptual-motor performance through training exercises would be valuable in its own right. The question is whether perceptual-motor problems are important in their own right, especially when the child's problem is that he is mentally retarded or has difficulty with learning.

The influence of Strauss and his thinking soon made itself felt in another area: work with cerebral palsied children. Here it was William Cruickshank who played a central role in demonstrating that these children, whose brains are indeed damaged, display the kind of performance deficits observed by Strauss in presumably brain-damaged, retarded children. Cruickshank and his students reported that children of average or above average intelligence who suffered from cerebral palsy display difficulties on tasks requiring visual-motor integration. In view of the fact that cerebral palsy is an affliction involving the portion of the brain which controls motor activity, a deficit on tasks requiring motor responses is hardly surprising. Whether the observed difficulties can be interpreted as involving figure-ground perception, as Cruickshank suggested, is thus open to question. This is not to cavil with a well-known authority or to detract from his important contributions to special education, but since Cruickshank views his work with the cerebral palsied (who are of normal intelligence) as a bridge between the research of Strauss with the retarded and later studies of learning-disabled children, the adequacy of this bridge merits scrutiny.

The bridge between the mentally retarded, the cerebral palsied, and the learning disabled has been used to carry two conceptual loads. One is the suggestion that learning-disabled children who display performance deficits on perceptual-motor tasks have something wrong with their brain. Strauss made that assertion for the retarded he had studied and Cruickshank thought he had confirmed it with his cerebral palsied.

The other conceptual load involves a widely used treatment-training procedure. Children with cerebral palsy have an impairment in their muscular-motor control and many of them can derive benefit from exercises designed to improve this control. This leads to the conceptual leap by which motor exercises are prescribed for learning-disabled children in the form of perceptual-motor training. Those who advocate these training exercises rarely spell out the theoretical rationale for their approach, but if they did it would in some fuzzy way lead back to work with the cerebral palsied and studies of the mentally retarded with assumptions about brain damage as the connecting link. With this weak conceptual basis, it is not surprising that nobody has ever demonstrated that perceptual-motor training improves the learning ability of learning-disabled children. When a child is having trouble learning academic subject matter in the classroom, it is of little help to him to become skilled in balancing on a walking beam or in tracking a moving object with his finger.

Newell Kephart, who also worked with Strauss at the Wayne County Training School, is another pioneer in the area of learning disabilities whose contribution is focused on perceptual-motor functions. He too came to the field of learning disabilities from a prior concern with brain-injured, retarded children. Many of the teaching methods and training procedures he recommended in his influential book, *The Slow Learner in the Classroom,* were based on work with such children. He stressed the interrelationship between perceptual and motor processes and emphasized that these go hand in hand in the course of a child's development. If a child has difficulty in the perceptual realm, it reflects an inadequacy in motor development. From this it follows that motor exercises, closely matched with perceptual experiences, are the means of helping such a child. Awareness of his own body, its parts and how these move, and the ability to distinguish between the left and the right side of the body were, to Kephart, essential prerequisites to learning directionality in space. Before a child can be expected to tell *b* from *d,* Kephart said, he must have acquired laterality with respect to his own body.

As the child changes the position of his own body with respect to the world around him, he comes to experience that world in relation to his body. Motor movements and sensory input are thus closely linked, and perceptual-motor development, no doubt, is an interrelated unity. If one separates perceptual development from motor development, or speaks of one without reference to the other, one ignores this unity. It is similarly artificial to say that motor development precedes perceptual development or to insist that motor training must take precedence over perceptual training when a child lacks perceptual-motor abilities. The relative emphasis on one or the other of these interrelated skills is sometimes a function of the professional background of the person who is contributing to this field. Thus, Kephart, having worked with children whose motor abilities were impaired by cerebral palsy, placed primary stress on motor exercises. For him, motor development preceded perceptual development. On the other hand, the optometrist Getman saw perceptual-motor difficulties primarily in terms of perceptual problems.

The people mentioned thus far have brought to the study of the learning-disabled child an orientation which depended heavily on the professional experiences they had before they turned their attention to this area. The early stress on brain damage and brain dysfunction and the still current emphasis on perceptual-motor training can be understood in these historical terms, though whether these approaches help the learning-disabled child remains to be seen.

The Test Makers

When a person has a physical illness that is difficult to diagnose, the physician will usually order a series of laboratory tests to aid in ascertaining the nature of the illness and to help in planning the treatment. This model has, unfortunately, been adopted by many educators who, faced with a child who can't learn, send such a child off to someone else to "get him tested." Used in this fashion, psychological tests often become not the means to an end but an end in themselves because, once the test results are in, nothing else is done for the child. Psychological tests have their place and psychologists who developed these tests have made important contributions, but in the schools they have assumed an importance that is quite out of proportion to what they can accomplish. Many teachers look to tests to give them answers which their own observations could probably give them not only better, but also more quickly.

The field of learning disabilities is plagued by an overreliance on tests. One of these tests, the Marianne Frostig Developmental Test of Visual Perception, reflects its originator's assumption that children with learning problems have difficulties in the area of visual perception. It grew out of Frostig's experiences with children enrolled in the Marianne Frostig Center of Educational Therapy, a Los Angeles institution she founded and has directed since 1948. The test evaluates such visual abilities as figure-ground perception, eye-motor coordination, and perception of spatial relations. Whatever weaknesses may be detected by this test are supposed to be attacked by a coordinated remedial procedure called the Frostig Program for the Development of Visual Perception.

Test and program thus form a package that leads to the temptation to find a deficit by using the test, remediate this deficit with the program, and evaluate the remediation with the test. In other words, one risks being captured in a circularity where the goal of intervention is improved test performance instead of improvement in the learning problem that prompted one to give the test in the first place. Unfortunately neither test nor program has stood up under the scrutiny of carefully controlled research. The test does not seem to test what it is supposed to test; the program does not seem to result in improved perceptual performance; and neither test nor program seems to bear much relationship to the academic learning problems of children with whom we are here concerned. Unaffected by this lack of a sound foundation, test and program continue to enjoy great popularity among educators.

A somewhat similar state of affairs exists with respect to another test that is frequently used by people seeking to find out "what is wrong" with a learning-disabled child. This test was originally devised to assess the language and communication problems of the mildly retarded child, was later applied in studies of culturally disadvantaged children, and has only lately become a favored tool in the field of learning disabilities. It is the Illinois Test of Psycholinguistic Abilities (ITPA), developed by Samuel Kirk, a pioneer in the field of learning disabilities who, in fact, gave the field its name.

While Frostig stresses visual development, Kirk is primarily interested in the reception, processing, and production of language. Unlike Frostig's intuitive, pragmatic approach to the construction of her test, Kirk and his students based the development of the ITPA on a theoretical model of language which had been devised by Charles Osgood and which had been rather well received in the 1950s. Meanwhile, however, the field of psycholinguistics has moved considerably beyond Osgood's early model, but the test which derived from it continues to live an autonomous existence, again despite the fact that research supporting its usefulness is, at best, inconclusive. As with the Frostig, there is a tendency to assess a child's weaknesses with the ITPA, to teach the child specific skills in which he is shown to be weak, and to assess the effectiveness of the intervention by once more administering the test. Whether this does anything for the child's learning somehow seems to be a question few care to ask.

Speaking of Language

When solutions to a problem, such as learning disabilities, are sought in an investigator's theorizing, it is very likely that the direction where the solution is expected to lie will be greatly influenced by that investigator's personal background and professional experience. We have thus seen how prior work with brain-damaged adults, with the profoundly retarded, or with culturally disadvantaged children led pioneers like Strauss, Kephart, and Kirk to their particular formulations regarding learning-disabled children.

Profoundly retarded, institutionalized children and adults are grossly limited in their use of language. Those working with them are thus rarely interested in studying language functions. Learning-disability specialists whose background was with such mental retardates have, therefore, usually deemphasized language skills, choosing instead to focus on perceptual and motor functions. Kirk's original interest in verbal communication skills derived from the fact that he had worked with mildly retarded preschool children who were not in institutions and for whom language was thus an important skill to master.

We close this brief historical review by mentioning two more of the early pioneers in the field of learning disabilities whose approach also reflects their previous involvement in other fields.

Helmer Myklebust had worked with the deaf. Such work forces one to focus on language and language acquisition. When Myklebust turned his interest to children with learning disabilities, one of his objects of study became the relationship of language to various disorders of learning. Work with the deaf, however, not only forces one to focus on communication skills, it also gives one an orientation to seeking physical causes of psychological problems. Deafness is, after all, caused by a defect located either in the ear, or in the brain, or in the nerves which conduct impulses between the two. One of the first questions a person who works with a deaf child must ask regards the physical nature of the condition.

Considering his background, it is not difficult to understand why Myklebust is among the most neurologically oriented of the pioneers in the field of learning disabilities. He coined the term *psychoneurological learning disability* and unhesitatingly attributes this condition to a dysfunction in the brain. His writings reflect a preoccupation with brain functions, neurological concepts, and questions of accurate diagnosis, but when he turns to questions of educational practices his recommendations are vague and nonspecific.

The last of the early contributors to the field of learning disabilities we shall here mention is Katrina de Hirsch, whose original specialty was speech pathology. She is primarily interested in reading disabilities and language disturbances and she argues—again in keeping with her background—that reading problems are primarily language problems which are caused by maturational dysfunctions. As remedial methods de Hirsch advocates the use of language training and perceptual-motor exercises. One might wonder how a person whose background was in speech pathology came to view perceptual-motor training as a method of treating reading disabilities. Was it a result of the fact that de Hirsch had once been exposed to the teaching of Kurt Goldstein in Frankfurt am Main, which is where our tale began?

Chapter 3

WHAT IS LEARNING?

Why is it so difficult to come to grips with the problem of learning disability? Why are there almost as many theories as there are experts and why can't they come to an agreement? Why has there been so little research that even today most teaching methods are based more on hunch than on fact?

There are many answers to these questions but one of the most important is that nobody really knows what learning is. It is therefore not surprising that nobody really knows what a learning disability is. Before one can hope to understand a condition in which learning *is not* taking place, one must know how to tell when learning *is* taking place. But learning is a curious concept.

We All Know What Is Meant by "Learning"

Or Do We? The word *learning* is a familiar term, used in everyday language. Everybody presumably knows what is meant by learning, but a moment's reflection reveals that the word eludes ready definition. To say with the dictionary that learning is the acquisition of knowledge or skill does not go very far in helping us say what we mean by learning. How is such knowledge or skill acquired, and when can we tell when acquisition has taken place or—crucial in discussing learning disabilities—has failed to take place?

The reason for this dilemma is that learning is not a thing to which one can point. It is not an activity that can be defined in terms of a direct observation. Eating can be defined in such a way. We can say that eating is the process of placing food in one's mouth and swallowing. One can point to a person who is engaged in this activity and all observers will agree that this person is eating. Now substitute learning in this example. Is it learning when a child looks at a printed page in a book? What would one point to in order to show someone what we mean by learning?

THE MIRACLE OF LEARNING

None of us are born with the ability to ride a bicycle. Nor will the skill develop in the course of growing older. One cannot even acquire the ability to ride a bicycle by watching others or by attempting bicycle riding by trial and error. What is more, one cannot learn to ride a bicycle by hearing someone tell how to do it or by reading about it in a book. Riding a bicycle is something we have to learn by having somebody teach us in a very direct and concrete way. Like other fathers, Judy's dad knew all this. So, he went out into the park one Saturday with the laudable intention of teaching his daughter to ride the bicycle she had been given for her fifth birthday.

Like countless fathers, mothers, big sisters, and older brothers before him, Judy's dad held on to the saddle and, with Judy on top, ran along as daughter pedaled and steered. Saturday passed and Sunday came and went. Aside from a tired Dad and a frustrated Judy, there was little they had to show for two days of practice. The moment Dad would let go of the saddle, Judy tipped over, unable to maintain her balance. The daylight hours after Dad came home from work and the following weekend were again devoted to the enterprise, for Judy was as determined to learn as Dad was intent on teaching. At the end of a Saturday afternoon, three weeks after they had started the procedure, success was still not in sight. Judy went to bed discouraged and Dad collapsed in his chair exhausted. That night Judy had a dream. She dreamed that she was riding her bicycle all by herself.

Sunday morning, with Dad standing by in amazement, Judy got on her bicycle and rode it triumphantly down the street. Miraculously she had learned to ride her bicycle while sleeping. What had happened? We can speculate about it, but we really don't know.

Learning is something that goes on inside a person and we can't watch it as it happens. We can only see the results, not the process of learning, and so it continues to have the awe-inspiring quality of a miracle.

Learning Is a Concept. Learning is not a thing to which one can point. It is an abstraction, a concept, a construct people have invented and then labeled with a word in order to have an easy way of communicating. Learning is presumably something that goes on inside a person's head; hence it is not something to which one can point: it is a covert process, like digestion, not an overt action, like eating.

Not only is learning a covert process, it is also a process of change over time. As such the operation of this process can be studied only indirectly through the observation of changes in performance over time. Digestion, too, is a covert process that involves change over time, but digestion can be studied if one has the right kind of laboratory equipment. One can trace for the absorption of various substances into the bloodstream. But in digestion we are dealing with physical substances; in learning we are dealing with skills and knowledge and that is where the analogy breaks down. In order to study learning one must identify a given activity that requires skill or knowledge for its performance, find a way to measure how well that activity is performed, and then record an improvement in that performance over time. Under certain circumstances (and that phrase has a lot of implications which we shall take up later), one can afterwards say that the change one observed was due to learning. Learning, then, cannot be observed while it is going on, only after it has taken place, and this may be why we know so much more about stomach ailments than about learning problems.

Learning Is a Description. The word learning stands for a process of change; it is no more than a description. If one forgets that fact, one can easily fall into a logical trap by assuming that the description can serve as an explanation. Take, for example, the observation that a boy who yesterday was unable to multiply 7 times 7, today gives the correct answer when presented with the same problem. One might now ask why he is able to do today what he was unable to do yesterday and come up with the answer, "Because he has learned this fact." Obviously, nothing has been explained. Learning is but a descriptive term we use when we observe an increase in skill or knowledge; to explain that observation by its description gains us nothing. It is circular. The circularity is immediately apparent if one asks people who thus have "explained" the improved performance how they know that learning has taken place. They will have to fall back on the very observation they had sought to explain in the first place.

The same problem obtains in the careless application of terms like learning disability if they are used simply as a description of an observed failure to learn. To observe that a child fails to learn and to ask, "Why?" answering with, "Because he is learning disabled" gains us (and the child) nothing. Nothing, that is, unless the term learning disabled stands for more than the simple observation because we have agreed to define it in such a fashion that it has additional implications. In Chapter 1 we presented a definition that does just that, so that, as used there, the term learning disability is more than a simple description.

How Can One Tell that a Child Is Learning?

Under certain circumstances, we said earlier, a change in skill or knowledge can be attributed to learning, and we promised to return to the implications of the phrase "under certain circumstances." What are these circumstances?

One of these circumstances is that what we observed did indeed represent an increase in the child's ability to solve a given problem or handle a given task. The child must have changed from not knowing to knowing, from inability to ability. How can one tell? We need some way of measuring the skill or knowledge in question and here the pitfalls are many. When we ask, "Was there *indeed* an increase in knowledge? Was the change *real?*," we are asking a question about the validity of the observation. Let us examine this issue in some detail because it is crucial in any discussion of learning and learning failure.

In order to demonstrate learning one must have a measure of the child's performance at two points in time. One must first record a condition of inability, later a state of ability. One must give a pretest and a posttest. The validity of a test has to do with its ability to measure what it is supposed to measure; it must tell the truth and it must do so consistently, otherwise it can't be trusted.

Let us assume that for a pretest a child is asked, "How much is seven times seven?" and she replies, "I don't know." Are we justified in assuming that she does not have the knowledge needed to give the correct answer? Would she be able to give the correct answer if another person asked her at another time or if the question were presented in writing or in a different language? If, for a posttest, we were to ask this girl the same question on the following day and she answered, "Forty-nine," can we be sure that this reflects an increase in her knowledge; or has someone just whispered the answer to her; or did she already know the answer yesterday but, for some reason, fail to tell us? For that matter, should the girl again reply that she does not know the answer, can we be really certain that she has failed to learn? Or did she learn but refuses to tell us; or did she know yesterday and knows today but keeps that knowledge to herself? Before one can draw any conclusions about learning, one must be certain that one has a valid measuring instrument. That is one of the circumstances.

The second circumstance that must be present if one is to attribute a change in performance to learning is that certain events have taken place between the two points of observation—between pretest and posttest—to which one can attribute the increase in knowledge. These events are opportunities for the child to acquire the knowledge in question. Learning, in other words, requires an opportunity to learn. If no such opportunity was present but we detect an increase in knowledge from pretest to posttest, we cannot attribute this change to learning. It is highly unlikely that the child spontaneously came by the knowledge that 7 times 7 is 49. It is more likely that the pretest failed to give us an accurate assessment of her actual knowledge; the child may have known at the time but failed to remember the answer until the posttest. Remembering a previously known fact is not learning. Nor is it learning when, as in the case of some simple motor skills, the passage of time permits the development of muscular coordination without additional practice. A child might not be able to hold a crayon at pretest but be able to do so at posttest a few weeks later. We'd call this maturation, not learning.

Opportunities to acquire knowledge usually take the form of someone engaging in behavior we call teaching. In the realm of motor skills, however, opportunities for learning can also be provided by chances to engage in trial and error practice. Here, the child is essentially his or her own teacher. In many instances, maturation and learning must go hand in hand if skill or knowledge is to increase. It should be obvious that a certain maturational level must have been reached if the exposure to a teacher or to trial and error practice is to result in learning.

Not only must a child have reached an appropriate maturational level in order to benefit from a teaching effort; the teaching must also be appropriate to the child's physical condition and to the skill level he or she has attained as a result of previous learning. It is important to point this out because it happens all too frequently that someone attempts to teach something to a pupil who is either maturationally or experientially unprepared to make use of this opportunity to learn. A physically or psychologically immature child, a child who has not had the opportunity to acquire prerequisite knowledge, or a child who speaks a language that is different from the language the teacher uses is not a child who can be expected to acquire the skill or knowledge being taught. To call such a child learning disabled is to ignore that the opportunity to acquire the knowledge being taught was, in fact, not provided.

At the beginning of this section we posed the question, "How can one tell that a child is learning?" Thus far we have said that to be able to say that learning has taken place, one must have a valid measure that reflects a lack of knowledge. This must be followed by an opportunity to acquire that knowledge, after which one must again have a valid measure which can show whether the previously missing knowledge is now available. Given that the tests we are using are indeed valid and measuring what they are supposed to measure, they should give us an answer to the question about learning. Unfortunately, however, it is very difficult to establish whether a test of learning is a valid test for the very reason that learning is an abstraction. There is a baffling circularity here, for if learning can only be demonstrated through the comparison of two test results, how is one to demonstrate that the tests being used are indeed testing learning? One would need an independent way of demonstrating learning. It would be nice if learning not only changed performance on tests but also increased the weight of the learner's brain. We could then weigh his brain before and after learning and thus ascertain the validity of our performance tests. This, however, is only a fantasy. There is no way of demonstrating learning that is independent of tests of performance. For that reason, there is no way in which one can establish the absolute validity of a test of learning. Since learning itself is an inference, tests of learning must always remain inferential.

To complicate matters even more, there is the issue of what constitutes a *meaningful* test of learning. Since the only thing we can observe is the child's performance, learning itself being a process we infer from that observation, what performance should one look for? The performance must clearly be relevant to the skill or knowledge that interests us. In the case of motor skill this does not pose much of a problem. If we want to teach a girl to tie her shoelaces, the criterion of whether she has learned is that she can perform the act of tying her shoes. But if we want to have a child learn to read, what shall be the criterion? Is it enough if the child can look at a sentence and say the words correctly? Is that *reading?* It is quite possible to do a limited amount of this by simply memorizing the words while listening to someone else reading from that page. This may be learning, but is it learning to read? One is reminded of the youngster who "reads" quite correctly while holding the book upside down. Such a child may even know the meaning of the words recited, but still that performance is not reading. Reading, after all, involves the ability to extract meaning directly from the written word; just saying the word aloud is not reading. To test whether a child has learned to read one must therefore have a test that requires the correct saying of words and permits the demonstration that the meaning of these words has been understood. With the possibility for imitation or prior memorizing ruled out, such a performance can tell us with a fair degree of assurance that the skill of reading has actually been acquired.

How Can One Tell that a Child Is Not Learning?

Even with all these complications, it is far easier to demonstrate that learning *has* taken place than to prove that learning has *not* taken place. Yet it is the latter we must be able to do if we are to speak legitimately about learning failures. The problem is basically one of logic, the logic of demonstrating the absence of something. If we meet a friend at a large party, held in a house with many rooms, and we ask, "Is Jack here?," the friend can readily answer in the affirmative if she has seen Jack. If she has not seen him, she cannot legitimately say, "No" unless she knows that he is in another house. Barring that, the careful answer for her to give is, "I have not see him." He might be at the party, but in one of the other rooms.

Failure to observe something does not mean that it does not exist; we may simply not have been able to observe it. Failure to demonstrate learning does not prove that learning has not taken place. In order to prove that something does not exist or that something has not taken place, one must exhaust all conceivable observations under all conceivable conditions. This always leaves room for the possibility that there is one observation or one condition that one has not thought of. In the case of learning, a different combination or type of pre- and post-test might have reflected improvement; the child might have learned but, for some reason, did not demonstrate this through changes in the performance we used as our test.

When one speaks of learning disability, however, one is saying more than that a child has failed to learn. The term learning disability carries the implication that the child is not able to learn. Thus, even when our tests show that a child has not learned something that someone has tried to teach, how can we be certain that the child is unable to learn? Have we looked in all conceivable places, used all conceivable conditions? How does one demonstrate that no learning is taking place? A child may fail to learn under one teaching method, but under some other teaching method this child might conceivably learn very well. What if that teaching method has not been tried or, for that matter, what if that teaching method has not yet been invented? Is one ever justified in saying that such a child "has" a learning disability?

The best one can ever do is to say that a child fails to reflect learning through changes in performance under the ordinary teaching methods which have been tried thus far. We know that children who are presumed to have learning disabilities are able to learn when specialized teaching methods are introduced. Is a learning-disabled child who learns under specialized teaching still a learning-disabled child? Or is a learning-disabled child simply a child in need of specialized teaching? The definition offered in Chapter 1 includes a statement about the child's need for specialized teaching, for there is no such *thing* as learning disability. It is no more than a label we apply to children who have special teaching needs. Learning disability is not an immutable entity that somehow exists in its own right. What we must therefore demonstrate is not that a child cannot learn but that the child has difficulty learning under circumstances where learning would ordinarily be expected to take place. What are these circumstances?

When Should a Child Be Learning?

Under what circumstances can one expect that learning should take place? The answer to this question lies in the appropriateness of the match between what the teacher seeks to accomplish and what the child is able to achieve—a match between the teaching or training efforts, on the one hand, and the child's capacity to benefit from these, on the other. The teacher's efforts must be appropriate for the child at any given moment. This means that one must take into account not only the child's developmental and physical state, his ability level and what he has learned in the past, but also his current condition. One obviously cannot speak of a learning difficulty if the child has a physical defect, such as poor vision, which unknown to the teacher, makes it impossible for him to clearly see the visually presented material in front of him. Nor would one designate as a learning disability the problems faced by a child whose teacher expects him to learn a skill which he is several years too young to master.

Again, it is not a learning disability if a mentally retarded child fails to benefit from instructions gauged for a child of average intelligence. One would not speak of a learning disability if mastery of material being taught presupposes prior learning which the child had no opportunity to acquire. The acquisition of reading, for example, presupposes that the child has been exposed to and has learned the language that is symbolized in the writing. A child who has grown up in an environment that is largely nonverbal or uses a different language would be expected to experience difficulty decoding written symbols into a language with which he has no familiarity. Lastly, it is incorrect to speak of learning disability if the child's current condition precludes learning. This not only means that one should not expect much learning from a child who is ill, or tired, or undernourished, or emotionally upset; it also means that the conditions are not right for learning if the child is not motivated to learn the material the teacher is trying to teach. In all of these instances we must first establish the conditions for learning before we can expect teaching to be effective. To repeat: there must be a match between the teaching or training efforts, on the one hand, and the child's capacity to benefit from these, on the other.

When one speaks of the appropriateness of the match between teaching efforts and the child's capacity, one places tremendous responsibility on those who teach. There are great individual differences in the way children learn and good teaching takes these differences into account. It is all too easy to seek vindication for a teacher's inability to teach a child by saying that the child has a learning difficulty when, in reality, the difficulty is not the child's but the teacher's. Only when a child fails to learn under conditions where other children of his age, intelligence, background, and potential are able to learn should one raise the question whether such a child might benefit from being called learning disabled.

Benefit from being called learning disabled? There is no point attaching a label to a child unless that label is somehow of help to the child. Most labels benefit those who do the labeling. They are often quick (but insufficient) explanations of things that puzzle us; they are handy administrative devices that permit us to say how many of each "type" of child we have in our schools; they often give us an excuse for our own inadequacies ("I can't be expected to teach him; he is retarded").

The label learning disabled is of benefit to a child when that label provides access to specialized teaching methods that the school reserves for those with that label. Although every child ought to receive *special* education in the sense of an education that suits his or her particular needs, we tend to reserve such education for those who have been singled out by a label, such as learning disabled.

Potential and Achievement

A learning difficulty represents a discrepancy between what we assume a child to be capable of learning under ordinary classroom conditions (the potential), and what that child actually learns (the achievement). To speak about a learning difficulty one must therefore be able to determine what a child *ought* to be learning. One must seek to establish the potential. How does one do that?

It is difficult enough to tell whether someone has learned something and, as we pointed out, even more difficult to determine that someone has *not* yet learned something. When it comes to finding out exactly how much someone *ought* to be able to learn, we are faced with a task that is impossible. Impossible, because it entails predicting the future. What we seek is a statement about a child's potential and potential entails something that lies ahead. As such, it is as impossible to measure potential as it is to measure tomorrow's temperature. We can estimate ("predict") tomorrow's temperature but we must wait until tomorrow before we can actually measure it. Similarly, we can estimate a child's potential but we must wait until later before we can know the accuracy of that estimate.

When one predicts tomorrow's temperature, the prediction has no influence on the weather. Yet if one predicts a child's future achievement on the basis of an estimate of his or her potential, one often influences the outcome which one is predicting. If I say that a given boy has low potential, teachers may not try very hard to teach him; if I say that a given girl has high potential, teachers may redouble their efforts. Such a self-fulfilling prophecy can be avoided only if I keep my prediction to myself. But what is the sense of predicting a child's potential if one does not base some educational action on what has been predicted? This is a dilemma of which one who predicts a child's low potential must be particularly aware, lest the prediction itself determine the outcome.

How then does one estimate a child's learning potential? The usual but illusory mode is to analyze the child's performance on a standard test of intelligence. This is done on the assumption that the child's level of intelligence, as shown in the intelligence test performance, bears some relationship to the child's learning potential. If the child's test score is near average or above average, it is assumed that he or she can benefit from ordinary classroom instruction. If that assumption is not met, if the child is not learning, one concludes that one has demonstrated a discrepancy between potential and performance, hence a learning disability.

This reasoning would be valid if intelligence tests did indeed measure intellectual potential, but this no test can do. An intelligence test is no more than a measure of performance on tasks where prior learning materially affects how well or how poorly one does. If one has been able to learn many things in the past, one is able to do better on a test of intelligence than if one has learned only a few things. But, doing well on such a test also means that one is able to put to use the things one has learned when they are called for by the test. In other words, what an intelligence test measures is how much of what a child has learned in the past he or she is able to display at the time of testing. This makes an intelligence test little more than a test of attainment or achievement.

It so happens that with normal children a score on an intelligence test is a rather good predictor of later school achievement, but this is not because the tests gauge "native intelligence" (whatever that is) but because the best predictor of future behavior is past behavior. That is to say, a child who has learned well in the past and can thus earn a high score on an intelligence test is likely to continue to learn well in the future—to achieve well in school. Conversely, a child who has learned little in the past (for whatever reason) will obtain a low score on an intelligence test and will—without changes in teaching methods—continue to learn little in the future. There is a dangerous pitfall in this relationship between test score and school performance, for if a low test score is taken at face value as a predictor of future school achievement, one is likely to write the child off as unable to learn (because of low intelligence) thus, assigning him to an academic setting in which little is expected of him. Since, in such a setting, the child is unlikely to learn much, the "prediction" is verified—another version of the self-fulfilling prophecy.

Take now the case of a learning-disabled boy. Suppose such a child has been unable to benefit from classroom instruction and has learned far less than he might have if instruction, taking his particular disability into account, had been specialized. When this child is given an intelligence test, his score will be low because his lack of prior learning will be reflected in his test performance. Since the low intelligence test score will go along with his low achievement level, the potential-performance discrepancy will not be manifested and the poor school performance might thus be ascribed to the child's low intelligence and the existing learning disability would be overlooked. Such an unsophisticated use of an intelligence test would result in writing off many children as "dull" who, in reality, have a learning disability which might be overcome if one instituted appropriate teaching methods. Nobody knows how many such undetected cases of learning-disabled children sit in the classrooms of our schools, victims of the notion that intelligence tests measure intelligence.

A somewhat more sophisticated approach to the use of intelligence tests in the assessment of intellectual potential is the analysis of consistencies and inconsistencies within the child's test performance. That is, one looks not merely at the score, as expressed in IQ points, but at the performance that led to this score. Individually administered tests of intelligence call for a variety of performances, ranging from the recall of general information to the assembly of puzzles. Since some of these tasks are less dependent on prior learning than others, a psychologist can attempt to estimate the child's "true potential" by looking for isolated evidence of good performance and assuming that this reflects what the child should be capable of doing.

Such an estimate, however, is only a guess, the accuracy of which is partly a function of the skill and experience of the psychologist. We shall return to this issue in Chapter 5.

How Does One Measure Achievement? The problem of identifying learning-disabled children does not only lie in the difficulty of estimating potential. Since one has to look for a discrepancy between potential and achievement, one not only needs a way of estimating the potential, one also needs a way of measuring achievement. This leads us back to the issue discussed earlier, the issue of assessing whether a child has learned something. School achievement is usually measured by so-called achievement tests, tests that purport to measure how much a child has learned in the various subject matter areas taught in school. These tests are standardized in such a way that a given child's scores can be compared to the average score expected for his particular grade level. Thus, a child can be below, above, or at grade level. Like all tests, achievement tests are subject to various distortions. An achievement test score should no more be taken as a measure of a child's "true achievement" than an intelligence test score should be viewed as reflecting "true intelligence."

What a child has learned may not be reflected on the achievement test. Such failure to substantiate learning that has occurred would result in a spurious discrepancy between the intelligence test score and the achievement test score. One would be wrong if one called such a child learning disabled. Conversely, though more rarely, a child's achievement test score might be spuriously high so that the potential-performance discrepancy would not emerge, thus masking an existing learning disability.

There is yet another factor that must be taken into consideration in a discussion of the assessment of learning disabilities. It is the general achievement level of the class or school in which a particular child is placed. If a child of average intelligence is placed in a class where the general achievement level and the teacher's expectations are unusually high, this child may seem to be performing quite poorly even though he or she is working at potential. Conversely, a child's relatively low performance due to a severe learning disability might go undetected if she has very high capacity but is placed in a low or low average classroom or school where teachers expect no more than the mediocre level at which this bright child is achieving. The relation of this to the socioeconomic class of the child's family should be apparent.

A Middle-Class Phenomenon? When the estimate of a child's potential is higher than his actual achievement in school, one can assume that such a child is an "underachiever," that his or her learning is being interfered with and, in the absence of other reasons, the existence of a learning disability should be considered. What kind of a child is likely to get to that point?

Someone must first have suspected that the child should be doing better in school. If, on a group administered intelligence test, the child achieved a low score, someone must have made the assumption that this test score did not reflect the child's true intellectual potential. Someone must then have seen to it that the child was given an individually administered test of intelligence since schools do not give these routinely. Finally, a skilled and experienced psychologist must have been involved. What kind of child is likely to have had all of these opportunities? It is, of course, the child of relatively sophisticated, educated parents who is attending a good school system. A child whose parents know enough not to accept the dullness explanation for their child's poor school performance. Parents who have the motivational and financial resources that will ultimately result in the identification of a learning disability. In other words, we are talking about the child of middle-class parents who take an interest in his education and who have the wherewithal to see to it that their child's interests are being served. With this bias built into the process of identifying learning-disabled children, it is not surprising that one finds references to an "epidemic of learning disabilities" among middle-class children. A thorough survey of all school children should reveal that this problem is not limited to one socioeconomic class.

Chapter 4

IS SOMETHING WRONG WITH THEIR BRAINS?

A Futile Assumption

Let it be said at the outset that there is no doubt that learning takes place in the brain. We can further agree that there are children with damaged brains who have trouble learning. The question we want to raise here is whether it makes sense to assume that learning-disabled children have something wrong with their brains. To ask whether it makes sense to make this assumption is, in fact, less important than to ask whether it helps such a child if one assumes that learning disability and brain disorder are related. It would assuredly help such a child if the assumption led us to employ effective remedial methods that we would not employ if the assumption had not been made. This, however, is not the case. There is nothing we do for a learning-disabled child that we would do differently if we made assumptions about brain damage, brain disorder, or brain dysfunction. The assumption contributes nothing of value as far as the child is concerned. On the contrary, since references to brain problems tend to give people ideas about irreversibility, permanence, and hopelessness, assumptions about brain problems tend to work against the best interests of the child.

Why is it then that notions about the brain continue to enter discussions of learning-disabled children? One answer to this lies in people's strong desire for explanations of things that puzzle them. It gives one a sense of certainty (albeit a false sense of certainty) to have an answer to the question why one's child has trouble learning. "Doctor, why does my child have trouble learning?" "Because he has minimal brain dysfunction." "Ah, thank you doctor; now I understand." Do you really?

The other answer to the question why speculations about brain disorders have persisted despite the absence of supporting facts lies in the difficulty that is inherent in doing research on this topic. The assertion that there is a causal relationship between learning disabilities and brain abnormality is very difficult to disprove. If the assertion were correct, if learning disabilities were caused by brain abnormalities, one should be able to show that there is no difference in terms of the performances which reflect learning between children with known brain damage and children with learning disabilities. Such studies have been conducted and the result has been that differences between the two groups *do* exist. Brain-damaged children perform in ways that are quite unlike those shown by the learning disabled. In other areas of science such results would refute the hypothesis. Not so in the realm of learning disabilities.

A CHILD WITH BRAIN DAMAGE

Paul was born with an impairment called spastic hemiplegia. Now seven years old, he still walks with a limp and uses his left hand very little, although he has become more efficient in the use of his left arm. He uses it to carry objects by pressing them against his body with his upper arm. His parents report that his behavior has improved over what it had been three years earlier. He now obeys better and can be trusted. He stays with the same activity for longer periods but still prefers rather simple toys. With them he repeats the same games without showing any inventiveness or originality. His parents also report that he has adjusted better to the household routine, and that he occasionally likes to help his mother in the house, such as putting things away for her. He becomes disturbed and difficult when routines are changed or irregularities occur.

Paul is at his best during the day when he is alone with his mother. In the afternoon, when his brother and neighbors return from school, he gets more tense and though he looks forward to seeing them, he usually ends up in tears because he pesters his brother and is left behind by children of his own age. The boy has had no formal schooling. While his mother has taught him some letters and numbers, she finds this difficult. She says that he seems to remember one day and forget the next. Paul cannot read, but he surprises his family with his ability to recognize brand packages and the labels of phonograph records.

In the summary of the results of a psychological examination, we read the following:

He continues to show verbal facility, but his actual name vocabulary is limited. . . . He expresses facts rather than thoughts. He comprehends simple, immediate, verbal connections . . . but not underlying thought processes. . . . His reasoning processes lack coherence and fail to integrate all given facts. . . . He has acquired information and academic skills (numbers and letters) which would place him on approximately kindergarten level. . . . Paul functions in the borderline defective range of intelligence. Though improved, his short attention span continues as one of his many liabilities. His tendency to respond to isolated stimuli in an immediate and uncontrollable fashion is reflected in his personal-social adjustments and accounts for labile reactions to the outside world. When he tries to avoid failure, he resorts to primitive attitudes. . . . In view of these findings, Paul should start only slowly on academic schooling. He would do rather poorly in academic competition and needs concessions to protect him from frustration as much as possible.

Adapted from E. M. Taylor, *Psychological appraisal of children with cerebral defects*, Cambridge, Mass., Harvard University Press, 1959, and used with permission.)

One White Crow. William James is reputed to have written that to upset the conclusion that all crows are black, there is no need to demonstrate that no crow is black; it is sufficient to produce one white crow. If one states that all learning-disabled children are brain damaged, the discovery of one learning-disabled child who is not brain damaged should refute the assertion. There is plenty of proof that learning-disabled and brain-damaged children are not the same—a white crow has been produced more than once—yet the minimal brain damage (MBD) hypothesis and similar theories persist. Why?

It is, of course, easy to agree on the definition of a crow and whether it is black or white. It is far more difficult to define brain damage, and learning disability, and appropriate performance measures. Hence, the persistence of the controversy. No matter how many studies refute the assertion that learning disability is caused by brain damage, those who make this assertion can always claim that one did not study the right children, examine the right variables, or apply the right measures; a different study, they allege, would show that they are right. It is a fatal flaw of this assertion that it cannot be put to a conclusive test. This in itself makes the assertion unscientific.

Another reason why the assertion that learning disability is caused by a brain disorder cannot be put to a conclusive test lies in the impossibility of conducting an experiment involving the manipulation of children's brain functions. To prove that one thing causes another, one has to introduce the presumed causal agent so as to be able to observe whether this leads to the predicted outcome. In the case of learning disability, one would have to take a group of normally learning children and produce a specific abnormality in their brains. If this led to learning disabilities, the causal hypothesis would be supported. It is obvious that nobody would perform such an experiment. Nor do we really know just what kind of brain abnormality one would have to produce in order to test the vaguely stated hypothesis about "minimal dysfunctions." For that matter, even an experiment of this nature would tell us only that brain damage *can* cause learning disability; it still would not prove that all learning disability is caused by brain damage.

When scientists are unable to perform an experiment because they are prevented by ethical or practical considerations, they sometimes rely on so-called experiments of nature. If one cannot intentionally damage a child's brain, why not study children whose brains have been damaged by illness or accident? The trouble with this is that the gross and often nonspecific damages sustained by these children are often accompanied by many features, such as the trauma of the accident and lengthy hospitalization, that might alone be responsible for the psychological changes one often observes. These changes, incidentally, rarely take the form of the kind of learning disability in which we are interested. Experiments of nature, in other words, do not support the hypothesis that learning disability is caused by brain damage.

If Not Damage, Then Maybe Dysfunction? Largely because nobody has ever been able to demonstrate that learning-disabled children have brain damage, the terminology has shifted to the term *minimal brain dysfunction syndrome.* Minimal, because it can't be demonstrated; dysfunction, because this says nothing about the structure of the brain, only that the brain is not working right; syndrome, because there is supposed to be a cluster of problems or symptoms that go together and form the learning-disability entity. What the phrase "minimal brain dysfunction syndrome" does, besides begging the question whether there is or is not something the matter with the brain, is to call upon an analogy from medicine to deal with a problem in education.

In medical diagnosis a syndrome is a cluster of symptoms, complaints, or difficulties which usually go together and identify a disease. Not all symptoms need necessarily be present in every instance, but they should coincide sufficiently often to present a consistent and recognizable picture. What are the difficulties which form the cluster labeled minimal brain dysfunction?

In medicine a syndrome is rarely made up of more than six or seven symptoms. For minimal brain dysfunction one authoritative list contained no fewer than ninety-nine problems. Some cluster! It is no doubt the result of different people calling different kinds of children learning disabled. When the problems of these children are then listed, the heterogeneity of the group is reflected in the vast number of problems. In any reasonably scientific and constructive classificatory scheme, one first defines a circumscribed entity and then observes its detailed characteristics. When this procedure is turned around, the category becomes a catchall wastebasket that helps no one, least of all the children who are thus labeled.

Of the multitude of problems presumed to be found in the

minimal brain dysfunction syndrome, some will occur more frequently than others. Those most often cited are, in order of frequency:

Hyperactivity

Perceptual-motor impairments

Emotional lability

General coordination deficits

Disorders of attention

Impulsivity

Disorders of memory and thinking

Specific learning disabilities: reading, arithmetic, writing, spelling

Disorders of speech and hearing

Equivocal neurological signs and electroencephalographic (EEG) irregularities

This list alone tells a lot about the notion of minimal brain dysfunction and its relationship to learning disabilities. If one starts out with the question, "What causes learning disability?" and answers, "Minimal brain dysfunction," should one not find learning disability to head the list of problems of children with minimal brain dysfunction? Instead, problems with school achievement are found in eighth place. Whatever minimal brain dysfunction might be, it is not the same thing as learning disability.

Another remarkable thing about that list is that the brain dysfunctions are so minimal that *equivocal* signs of neurological problems and irregularities (not abnormalities) in EEG patterns show up in tenth place. On the other hand, hyperactivity leads the list. Could it be that minimal brain dysfunction is no more than another word for hyperactivity and that learning disability is sometimes associated with that problem? If that is the case, what does the term minimal brain dysfunction contribute? It seems quite superfluous and only confuses the issue by placing emphasis on the brain in the complete absence of supporting evidence that this is where the cause of the problem is to be found.

Supporting evidence is indeed absent. When one examines with great care children with learning problems, as was done in a study conducted at the University of Iowa, one finds that the so-called symptoms of minimal brain dysfunction do not inter-relate in the way they should if they formed a syndrome. Nor do they seem to have anything to do with the quality of a child's school performance. In other words, minimal brain dysfunction is neither a syndrome nor an explanation of learning disability.

What about Hyperactivity?

Many discussions of learning-disabled children use the expression "hyperactivity" as if it were synonymous with learning disability or as if the two conditions were invariably found together. Neither is the case. Many children are hyperactive without being learning disabled; some learning-disabled children are also hyperactive. The relationship between the two conditions is not at all clear.

What is meant by the term *hyperactive?* No more than that someone has decided that the child so labeled moves about more than the observer deems normal. Since there is no standard by which one might judge the normal activity level of a child of a given age, the designation of hyperactive is based on many subjective factors. It has a lot to do with the expectations and tolerance level of the adults who judge a child's behavior. Like other behaviors that are classed together by a descriptive label, overly active behavior not only comes in many degrees of magnitude but is also likely to have several different causes. Since activity level is a normal human characteristic, it, like other characteristics, will vary from one individual to the next. Some people are short, some tall, many of medium size. One should not be surprised to find that some children are mildly lethargic, some quite active, and many somewhere in between. Just as we would not say that a person whose size is near the upper end of the normal range of height is therefore sick, so we should not attach a label which sounds like an illness to a child whose activity level is near the upper end of the normal range of body movement.

That is not to say that a child with a high activity level is easy to live with. Nor is it to say that there are not some children whose activity level is indeed of pathological magnitude. A man who is eight feet tall is also no longer in the normal range. We know further that children who have sustained damage to the brain through accident or illness sometimes develop hyperactivity. They had a normal activity level before and became hyperactive following the trauma. This acute beginning of the problem often sets them apart from the normal variant who will have been a handful for the parents from the start.

The fact that some children with known brain damage are found to be hyperactive has led some writers to the illogical conclusion that all hyperactive children must be brain damaged. They would further argue that, since many learning-disabled children are also hyperactive, learning disability must be caused by brain damage or, at least, be the result of minimal brain dysfunction. The logical fallacy in this reasoning is so blatant that one wonders how it can be maintained by so many bright and otherwise reasonable people.

The Squeaky Wheel. Let us examine the relationship between hyperactivity and learning disability. Why is it that these conditions are so often found to go together?

Learning disability, as we pointed out in Chapter 3, is difficult to detect because it can only be identified through a comparison of the child's actual performance with his or her estimated potential. As a result, a very bright boy with a learning disability may elude detection because he can function at an average level, keep up with his class, and thus not arouse anyone's suspicion that he could be doing much better work.

Imagine now two such learning-disabled boys in the same class. Neither is suspected of having a problem because both are living up to the expectations of their teacher. One of them, however, fails to sit still, is constantly on the move, fidgets, speaks out of turn, and occasionally hits other children. The teacher is distressed and eventually seeks outside help. The boy is thus singled out for study and in the process it may be discovered that, according to his intelligence test performance, he should be doing far better work in class. A discrepancy between his estimated potential and his actual performance has now been found and the term learning disabled enters the picture, joining the previously affixed label of hyperactive.

The other boy, the one who sits quietly doing average work and who, unbeknown to anyone, should be capable of much more, continues on as an undiscovered child with learning disability. If one multiplied this example sufficiently, one could arrive at the observation that all learning-disabled children are hyperactive—not because this is in fact the case, but because it is the hyperactive, learning-disabled child who calls attention to himself and thus comes to the notice of the people who staff specialty clinics and write articles for professional journals, articles which ultimately find their way into books.

The frequently reported coincidence of hyperactivity and learning disability may thus be the result of a bias in selection. Even for those cases, however, the fact that hyperactivity and learning disability occur together tells us nothing about the nature of that relationship. It is well to be aware that the observation of two events occurring together can throw no light on whether one causes the other. A correlation does not prove causation.

It can be observed, for example, that when it rains many people carry umbrellas and wear galoshes. But the wearing of galoshes does not cause umbrella carrying. Nor do umbrellas or galoshes cause the rain, despite the fact that the appearance of these items often precedes precipitation. In this instance, we happen to know the causal relationship and we can smirk at the naïveté of the woman from Venus or man from Mars who might view it otherwise. Yet when it comes to observing correlations between learning disability and hyperactivity, we often fall into this very trap. It may be that hyperactivity causes learning disability. Or it may be that both hyperactivity *and* learning disability are caused by some third factor. Or it may be that learning disability and the resulting experience of repeated failures makes children hyperactive. At this point we can do no more than speculate about the relationship.

In this connection it is interesting to note that in a survey of some 1,500 ten-year-old boys taken from the general population, the mothers reported in 42 percent of the cases that their child was restless and hated to sit still. It is conceivable that the so-called hyperactivity of learning-disabled children is no more than the troublesome but normal motility level that one should expect to find in some children simply as the result of the range of individual differences.

Does It Matter? One might ask why it matters so much to know the nature of the relationship between hyperactivity and learning disability. The answer is that what one does for, to, or with the child depends on one's view of this relationship. If the focus is on hyperactivity as the cause of learning disability, intervention is often aimed at reducing the hyperactivity on the untenable assumption that learning will take care of itself once the child "settles down." It is here that the prescription of medications, which we shall examine later, finds its use and abuse.

The reasoning begins with the assumption that hyperactivity is a symptom of a medical problem (brain dysfunction) and that it therefore calls for medical treatment. Despite its impressive sounding label, hyperactivity, or its even more ponderous synonym, hyperkinesis, this state is not a disease. The word hyperactivity is no more than a description of behavior, based on a judgment of what is "too much" activity. What is "too much" for one person or group of persons may be quite acceptable to others. Hyperactivity is thus essentially a relative, descriptive label which reflects other people's reactions to the child's behavior. There is no norm for what is the appropriate level of a child's motor activity other than that residing in the expectations of the social environment.

No doubt, a child who engages in a great deal of vigorous activity can be difficult to have around the house and annoying to have in a classroom. Such a child causes problems but that does not necessarily mean that they are his or her problems. In some instances at least, the problem may lie in the low tolerance level of the people in the child's environment. At times it may thus be worth considering whether intervention should be aimed at raising the tolerance level of significant adults instead of lowering the activity level of the child.

Some children are more active than other children. They are born that way and it is idle to speculate why this is the case. To speculate who is to blame is more than idle; it is destructive. Whenever a child has a problem or is, in some way, different from the way the parents had expected, the question of who is to blame frequently arises. This does nothing except to create friction, guilt, and uncertainty. The question should not be "who is to blame" but "what are we going to do about it?"

What to Do? Hyperactivity, as such, is not a problem. The problem lies in the effect high activity level has on the child's interaction with his environment. If parents are critical, disapproving, and punitive toward a child whose high activity level is annoying to them, the child may well react with insecurity, anxiety, and aggression. This can set up a vicious cycle that brings many such children and their parents to the attention of such helping professionals as psychologists and psychiatrists. Much grief could be avoided if parents were able to accept their child's activity level as a fact of life—as a characteristic of their child rather than as a problem that must be conquered or a disease that must be cured.

A child with an activity level that is higher than his or her parents might prefer needs to have an environment that takes that activity level into account. The physical arrangements in the home can be modified so as to create fewer occasions for conflict between the parents and the child. If a child were unusually short for his age, nobody would hesitate to give him a pillow to sit on so that he can sit at table with the rest of the family. Similar accommodations must be made for the highly active child. Since sitting still for long periods of time is difficult for such a child, occasions when sitting still is required can be segmented so that the periods are shorter. A long automobile trip, for example, can be broken up with frequent stops in recognition of the child's needs.

Like all children, but maybe more than most, the highly active child needs clear-cut and consistently enforced rules. Structure is the key word. He or she must know what goes and what does not go, must be able to count on knowing where the parents stand.

Since hyperactivity is not the principal topic of this book but comes to be mentioned only because it is often raised in the context of learning disabilities, we shall forgo a detailed discussion of what parents can do with and for a hyperactive child.

A reader who is interested in the issue of hyperactivity, per se, will find several books devoted to this topic listed in the Annotated References at the end of this book.

Drugs and Activity and Learning

Why Do We Know So Little? By now, almost everybody who is interested knows that hyperactivity can be reduced through the administration of stimulant drugs such as amphetamines or related medications, such as methylphenidate. They are better known by their commercial brand names, among which Dexedrine, Benzedrine, and Ritalin are the most familiar. As with so many other things that "everybody knows," what we know about these drugs and their effect on children is really quite limited. For one thing, they are not equally effective with all children. They help some, make others worse, and have no effect in a large number of cases. At some dosage levels, the drugs reduce a child's hyperactivity but also interfere with his learning, while at other levels certain kinds of rote learning are improved, but the hyperactivity remains unchanged. What is more, we really don't understand how these drugs exercise their effects, nor are we sure that they don't have long-range and undesirable side effects.

One of the reasons why we know relatively little about these drugs is that it is extremely difficult to carry out good research on these questions. Such research calls for large numbers of children with clearly defined and identical problems. It requires ways of measuring objectively whether the problem (hyperactivity) has changed. Some of the children in the study must be given the drug being investigated, while others must receive a *placebo,* a pseudomedication by which one controls for the psychological (as opposed to the pharmacological) effect of taking a pill. What is more, neither the child, nor the parents, nor the teacher, nor the person dispensing the pill must know whether it is the placebo or the real thing. The group receiving the drug must then go on placebo, while the group on placebo must go on the drug so that one can tell whether there is a sequence effect.

All this time, the children must be observed and evaluated—not only in terms of their behavior and learning but also regarding their physical condition. Unfortunately, many of the necessary tests, particularly those related to learning, lose their sensitivity with repeated administration. This calls for the use of alternate forms of these tests and this, in turn, demands that the order in which these forms are used must be carefully planned to avoid bias. Since all these procedures entail many clinic visits and child-physician contacts so that the amount of personal attention alone might be responsible for changes in behavior, there should also be a group of children who receive nothing but this personal attention in order to assess its effect. Finally, in order to learn about long-term effects of a drug one should, of course, follow the children in such a study for many years. Many of these refinements of research are often sacrificed for the sake of expediting the study or compromised for the sake of ethics or expediency. As a result, much of what is known about the treatment of hyperactive children with stimulant drugs is based on clinical trials or reports from less than adequate research.

What Does It Prove? Amphetamine-related drugs are central nervous system stimulants. The observation that they change the behavior of some hyperactive children has been used as "proof" that hyperactivity is caused by something that is wrong in the central nervous system. Those who view hyperactivity as a symptom of minimal brain dysfunction are particularly prone to accept this logical fallacy. One cannot argue from an observed effect to a prior cause. The fact that aspirin alleviates headaches does not prove that headaches are caused by a deficiency in the brain of aspirin's chemical ingredients.

Another version of this logical fallacy is the frequent practice of using the administration of a drug like Ritalin in order to "diagnose" minimal brain dysfunction. Because this elusive syndrome is difficult to identify, it has been advocated that hyperactive children be placed on a trial regimen of a stimulant drug in order to observe its effect. If such a child's activity level then shows a reduction, this is used as an argument that the hyperactivity was due to minimal brain dysfunction. All that this observation proves, of course, is that—for the children in question—the drug reduced activity level. What if normal children responded to this drug in the same way? Would this prove that these children, too, have minimal brain dysfunction? It turns out, of course, that nobody knows how normal children would react to this drug because (for obvious reasons) nobody has ever done a study in which normal children were given the drug in order to have them serve as a control group.

It would be unthinkable to pick a group of normal children from a classroom and to administer a potent chemical agent to them for the sake of studying its effect. Unthinkable, maybe, but isn't that what happens many times when children are "put on drugs" because someone, usually a teacher, has reported that they are hyperactive? Is it not likely that among such children are an unknown percentage who are essentially normal youngsters whose only problem is that they are more restless than their teachers or parents would like?

What Can One Conclude? Given that our knowledge about the effect of stimulant drugs on hyperactive children is limited by the difficulties that stand in the way of definitive research, what can one conclude? It seems that a small proportion of hyperactive children show prompt and rather dramatic improvement when they are first put on one of these drugs. Many more show some or even considerable change for the better. But some fail to respond and some even get worse. One also must keep in mind that stimulant drugs tend to suppress the appetites of many children and that some have been found to suffer a suppression of growth in both weight and height.

Thus far we have spoken only about the drug's effect on the child's motor activity, for the usual focus of such medication is on hyperactivity. What about learning? For children who are both learning disabled and hyperactive, it is not enough to demonstrate that their hyperactivity decreases. While this makes life easier for the teacher and parents of the child, the crucial question is whether the child's academic performance improves, that is, whether the learning disability is alleviated. It turns out that nobody has ever demonstrated that Ritalin or any other drug *produces* learning; only teaching can do that. With children for whom the hyperactivity and its associated behavior problems have prevented teaching from being effective, the effect of a carefully administered drug can make them better prepared to benefit from good teaching.

The positive effect of stimulant drugs is particularly pronounced in the performance of routinized, repetitive tasks that require lengthy periods of attention and relative immobility. The children seem to "settle down" and they look improved. They are often less impulsive, less aggressive, and less destructive, particularly in structured situations. Though their reasoning and problem-solving ability, as such, do not seem to improve, the children are more likely to stop and evaluate alternatives and their ability to concentrate on a task is improved.

These qualities will obviously facilitate learning provided what the child is being taught takes into account that prior to this improvement this child failed to acquire a great deal of basic and essential knowledge. No one should assume that such a child can now suddenly keep up with the class. A great deal of carefully planned remedial work may be needed before age-appropriate achievement can be expected. Not only is there likely to be a gap in the child's education that must be filled, the child may also have acquired attitudes about himself and about school and learning that may interfere with success unless they too are taken into account and dealt with.

The relationship between the effects of stimulant drugs on hyperactivity and their ability to facilitate learning is rather complicated. This is, in part, because changes in hyperactivity are rather gross while changes in readiness to learn are quite subtle. One can observe whether a child is sitting still; one cannot observe whether a child is learning. There is, furthermore, a relationship between the amount of a drug (the dosage level) a child is receiving and the effect of the drug. The dosage level must be adjusted by the physician for each individual child until the desired effect is achieved.

But what is the desired effect? Since the drug is primarily prescribed in order to reduce hyperactivity, the effect that will be looked for in the process of determining the appropriate dosage is change in the hyperactive behavior. The physician will obviously have to rely on reports from the parents and teachers regarding the child's behavior. Recent studies have shown that by the time parents and teachers report a noticeable reduction in hyperactivity a dosage level will have been reached that is so high as to interfere with clear thinking and problem solving. At very low dosage levels—so low that no changes in activity level can be noticed—stimulant drugs seem to enhance learning, but this effect disappears and is, in fact, reversed by the time changes in activity level can be observed.

Ideally, this would call for a compromise with the dosage level. Give the child just enough to reduce hyperactivity but not so much as to impair learning. Yet the "just enough" probably means that adults will have to be willing to put up with a good deal of fidgeting and moving about. This raises the question of what is more important to the adults, a quiet child or a learning child? Or are there ways of dealing with hyperactivity without resorting to drugs? Indeed there are. We shall review drug-free approaches in Chapter 7 for there are other pitfalls and dangers in the use of drugs which make a drug-free alternative all the more desirable.

When a child has lived through years during which adults have consistently complained about his or her unacceptable behavior and lack of school progress, a relatively sudden improvement brought about by taking a drug will have psychological consequences. Such children may well come to view themselves as unable to control their behavior and as needing a chemical agent to solve their problem and to get adults off their back. This may well pave the way for future resort to any of a variety of pills for solving problems of living.

Associated with this risk is the likelihood that a child who attributes a change in his or her behavior to the effects of a medication may become more dependent on the drug than the child who views the improvement as largely due to his or her own effort and achievement. That is, children who attribute improvements to a drug may require continued medication in order to maintain this improvement, while children who see the drug as merely a temporary crutch while they are learning to control their own behavior should be able to relinquish the drug at an earlier time. From this one can conclude that when drugs are used in cases of hyperactivity, the child must be given a clear understanding that this is a vehicle to *help him learn* to sit still, not something that will make the problem go away.

Potential Abuses

We cannot leave this topic without discussing some of the potential abuses of medications used with hyperactive children. Prescribing a drug is very easy. It takes but a few minutes of a physician's time to write a prescription, even less to have it renewed. Responsible practitioners will be careful to monitor the effect of the drug, not only to ascertain whether it brings about the desired improvement but also to make certain that there are no untoward side effects. This calls for careful examinations at repeated intervals, not merely an occasional telephone conversation with a parent.

But even the most careful medical practitioner has no control over the use of the drug once it is in the hands of the patient. Parents, school personnel, and at times even the children themselves must now make sure that the medication is taken regularly and in the proper dosage. It is disconcerting to hear reports of children who are given a double dose in order to make up for a pill taking that was missed or because they are "acting up" more than usual. Pills are sometimes given, without benefit of a physician's advice, to other children who, in the opinion of a parent or teacher, "need it." Children who carry their own medications to school have been known to trade, sell, or throw them away. These misuses, incidentally, are another reason why meaningful research on drug effectiveness is so difficult. How does one know whether children for whom the medication does not work or for whom it has undesirable side effects are actually receiving the dosage that has been prescribed? Supervision is very difficult.

Still another issue which must be raised in this connection is the effect widespread use of stimulant drugs for presumably medical reasons has on educational efforts to prevent drug abuse. On the one hand we tell our schoolchildren not to turn to drugs to solve personal problems. But in the very schools where marijuana is labeled a "chemical cop-out," a high percentage of children are told to take their pills so that they will behave and learn better. Considering the fact that we know no more about the long-range effects of continuous use of stimulant drugs than we do about marijuana, this double standard is both cynical and irresponsible.

Chapter 5

WHAT CAN ONE TELL FROM TESTS?

The puzzle created by a bright child who fails to learn, refuses to go to school, or encounters other problems related to school inevitably calls for an answer. What is the matter with the child? Is she emotionally disturbed? Brain damaged? Learning disabled? Does he have perceptual difficulties? School phobia? Dyslexia? Answers to such questions are often difficult to obtain. In looking for these answers, parents, teachers, and professional specialists often turn to psychological and educational tests in the hope that they can clarify the picture and point the way to what should be done.

What Tests Can Do—and What They Cannot Do

When a child has a puzzling illness, the physician is often helped in making a diagnosis by turning to a series of laboratory tests and physical examinations. Because tests help the physician diagnose a physical illness, we often hope that tests can help the educational specialist find the answer to a puzzling school problem. This, unfortunately, is not true. A child's learning problem is not the same thing as a physical illness. Psychological problems are not physical problems. The flawed analogy from physical illness to psychological problem is very misleading, and one source of the misplaced faith in psychological tests. The other source has been the promises made by psychologists which have resulted in their tests being greatly overrated.

THREE YEARS IN LIMBO—PART I

Mary Jane Bronkowsky was brought to the clinic when she was nine years old. She walked with a stooped, shuffling gait and breathed through her mouth, drooling saliva from her slack lower lip. When the psychologist tried to talk to her, she flexed her elbows and shook her hands in a fast, loose-wristed, fluttering movement. Her language consisted mostly of poorly pronounced, single expressions which often sounded more like grunts than words. Her mother reported that Mary Jane would at times hit the side of her head with her wrist in rapid, drumfire fashion, and that at other times she had been observed to press her fists into her eyes and to rub them with much vigor. All this behavior, according to her mother, had gradually developed over the past three years; before that Mary Jane had seemed like a bright child whose behavior was no different from that of other children in the neighborhood, and no different from that of her older brother when he had been her age. What had happened to Mary Jane?

It is risky to reconstruct a child's history in an attempt to trace the development of a problem, but in Mary Jane's case the facts seem fairly clear. When she was four years old, her parents enrolled her in the preschool program of their suburban school system. They then lived in a modest neighborhood, some 30 miles outside the large city where the girl's father, like many of the other men from the town, worked as a laborer in the steel industry. The local school system, supported from real estate taxes, had to fight each year to have the voters approve its budget. Teacher salaries were low and special services were practically nonexistent.

Mary Jane had apparently enjoyed the pasting-and-coloring activities of nursery school, but after two months the teacher informed Mrs. Bronkowsky that Mary Jane was having trouble keeping up with the class. She would run her crayon all over the page instead of staying within the outline of the picture to be colored. When the children were to jump, skip, and hop during "gym," Mary Jane would inevitably stumble in a clumsy fashion. As the child's mother wistfully said, "Mary Jane flunked skipping in nursery school." However, since Mary Jane seemed to like school and Mrs. Bronkowsky had started to work mornings in the local supermarket in order to supplement the family income, the parents decided to leave the girl in the program despite the teacher's suggestion that she might be too young and that it might be better to have her taken out and brought back the next year.

In kindergarten Mary Jane's difficulties became a source of greater concern. During the first parent-teacher conference in November, Mrs. Bronkowsky was told that Mary Jane should be tested because her attention span seemed much shorter than that of her peers; that she was unable to do the prereading exercises on which the class was working; and that there was much doubt that she would be ready for first grade the next year.

At the time, Mary Jane was a happy little girl who played age-appropriate games with her friends in the neighborhood and got along well with her older brother and younger sister. She had been, so her mother recalled, "a great mimic" who could imitate the characters in her favorite TV programs and would entertain the family by talking like Bugs Bunny.

Since the local school system could not afford professional services, the person who tested Mary Jane was not a trained psychologist but one of the teachers from junior high school who had taken some evening courses at the nearby university. The test results came as a shock to the Bronkowsky family. Mary Jane was said to have the intelligence of a borderline defective, to have perceptual-motor difficulties, and to be suffering from minimal brain damage. Placement in regular class was out of the question. Mary Jane was to be transferred to the "opportunity class" as soon as possible.

Under its nice sounding name, the opportunity class program was the school system's attempt at providing special education. Located in one of the two elementary schools, the program consisted of one class for children between five and nine, while another class held those above nine, including a few boys and girls who were fifteen and sixteen years old. These classes had to serve the needs of all children who for one reason or another were thought unable to benefit from regular classroom instruction. The room for the younger age group contained 28 children, cared for by one teacher. Some of these children were physically handicapped; others were retarded, autistic, emotionally disturbed, or hard of hearing. One child was blind. These were to be Mary Jane's classmates. The Bronkowskys were very upset, but not being the kind of people who question the opinions of "experts" or go counter to the recommendation of an authority, they had their child transferred to this opportunity class.

Intelligence. Psychologists have long been justly proud of their ability to measure. In fact, their field was established when its early pioneers succeeded in devising measures of sensation, perception, and memory. It is, however, one thing to be able to measure the smallest distance between two points that a person is able to discriminate when these are pressed against various places on the skin, or to count the number of nonsense syllables an individual is able to memorize in a given length of time; it is quite another to measure how much academic material a child should be able to learn in the next nine months or four years.

This, however, is precisely what psychologists set out to measure when they developed the first tests of intelligence. Alfred Binet, the French psychologist, had been given the task of selecting from among the schoolchildren of Paris those who were not likely to benefit from regular education because of what was then called feeblemindedness. The test he developed for this purpose became the ancestor of every intelligence test now in use, many of which base their claim to validity on the fact that their scores agree or correlate with the scores on "the Binet."

Over the years intelligence tests have been revised and refined, and the term *IQ* has entered the everyday vocabulary of people who have little or no idea what it really means. Even people who should know better sometimes think that a child's IQ is a measure of his or her "native intelligence." That is not the case. All an IQ represents is the score which the child received on the particular test from which the IQ is taken. The score may have been converted into a ratio that takes the child's age into account, or it may have undergone some statistical transformation so as to compare the child's score with the scores of other children of the same age, but basically it still represents no more than a score on a test. The score, in turn, represents the answers the child gave to the test items; it represents test performance—not native intelligence. The implication of this will become clear as we look at some of the test items from a very popular test of intelligence, the Revised Wechsler Intelligence Scale for Children, the WISC-R.

An intelligence test is designed to compare an individual child's performance with the performance of a theoretical "average child" of the same age. In order to do that, those who develop such tests must answer two important questions. What kind of performance is relevant to what I am trying to measure, and how do I ascertain the performance of the average child?

The answer to the first part of that question, what kind of performance is relevant, depends, of course, on how one has defined intelligence. Most people would agree that finding out how accurately a child can throw a dart at a dart board is not relevant to intelligence. That has to do with coordination and one would not want to include dart throwing in a test of intelligence. But what about drawing a circle, or completing a picture of a man, or tracing a maze? Most of us somehow view these tasks as having something to do with intelligence. In addition they have to do with coordinating muscular movements with visual perception. But so does dart throwing. There too, the child would have to see something and coordinate muscles in order to accomplish the task. Why then circle drawing, but not dart throwing? The answer lies in the fact that we have more or less arbitrarily decided that circle drawing has more to do with intelligence than dart throwing, possibly because circle drawing is similar to one of the things one is supposed to do in school: writing. It is the arbitrariness of this decision that must be noted. There is no such thing as intelligence; there is only an idea, a concept we have developed, something scientists call a hypothetical construct.

It is this arbitrariness that has led to the existence of any number of definitions of intelligence. Binet spoke of the ability to make and follow a plan, to adapt means to an end, and to be able to evaluate one's own performance. Wechsler, on the other hand, views intelligence as the overall capacity of people to cope with the world around them. It is, for him, a global entity that one can infer from observing how people react to the multitude of stimuli around them. The test he developed thus seeks to observe the child in a variety of situations requiring a variety of ways of coping with tasks. Intelligence, then, is best defined by a statement that sounds almost waggish: Intelligence is what intelligence tests test. Indeed, that is all it is. With different assumptions about intelligence we would have different tests.

Who Is the Average Child? After making the arbitrary decision of what tasks to use to observe a child's performance, the developer of an intelligence test must answer the other question: How does one find out how an "average child" would perform on the test? The average is a statistical myth, a number that is supposed to be representative of a series of different numbers. The average child, therefore, is also a myth. It is the child who is supposed to be representative of a large number of different children. What is done in practice to concretize this myth is to select a large number of children, give them the test one is developing, and obtain the average score of their performances. But how large a number of children does one need for this, and what kind of children should they be?

Wechsler selected 2,200 children ranging in age from six and one half to sixteen and one half. One hundred boys and 100 girls were chosen from each age level. They came from rural and urban areas; 85 percent were white, 15 percent were nonwhite; and the occupations of their parents (head of the household) as well as the region of the country where they lived was representative of the general population of the United States as established by the 1970 census.

What is of interest from the standpoint of the topics with which we are dealing in this book is that Wechsler's sample on which he standardized his test was limited to "normal" children. Children with severe emotional problems and those diagnosed and institutionalized as mental defectives were not included. Bilingual children were tested only if they could speak and understand English. Children suspected of being mental defectives were included if they lived at home.

The test performances of these 2,200 "normal" children are

thus the norm against which one compares the performance of an individual child who is given this test of intelligence. Children who do better than the 200 children in their age group are seen as having above average intelligence. If they do worse than the 200, their intelligence is below average. One question one should always ask when a child is to be classified on the basis of such a test is whether the comparison being made is, in fact, relevant. Only if the "average" child is indeed a representative of the child being tested does it make sense to make this comparison. A child who has trouble understanding English, or an institutionalized mental defective, or a child with a severe emotional problem did not have a representative among the standardization sample. The comparison with that sample may thus be irrelevant and therefore unfair.

If the best way to define intelligence is in terms of what intelligence tests test, then the best way to describe intelligence is to describe one of these tests. In doing this, we can explore the many ways in which a given child, particularly a learning-disabled child, may encounter difficulties which can result in a distortion of the information one can glean from the test. We thus turn to an examination of one of the most widely used tests of intelligence.

The Wechsler Intelligence Scale for Children—Revised

Wechsler's scale is composed of ten sections or subtests (plus two supplementary tests) which take from an hour to an hour and a half to administer. Five of the tests call for verbal responses; they make up the Verbal Scale. Five subtests involve things the child has to do with his or her hands; these compose the Performance Scale. The Verbal Scale and the Performance Scale are scored separately, thus resulting in a Verbal IQ, a Performance IQ, and a combined, Full Scale IQ. More of that later.

The Verbal Scale. This scale contains five subtests, plus one supplementary test which the examiner may either substitute for one of the other tests or add as a sixth measure. The subtests have names but these are not too revealing of their content. They are Information, Similarities, Arithmetic, Vocabulary, and Comprehension. As we discuss some typical items from each of these scales, we shall see that correct answers—that is, high scores—depend on much more than whatever it is that we call intelligence. (In order to preserve the security of the test, the examples given here are not actual test items but highly similar problems.)

One of the items from the Information subtest reads something like this: "Who invented the telephone?" The child who can answer this question correctly earns one point. The child who fails this question earns nothing. What are some of the conditions that would enable a child to earn a point on this item? The child must attend to the question, hear it correctly, and understand what it means. That is, he or she must know the meaning of words like "invented" and "telephone." The child must have had an opportunity in the past to have acquired the necessary information, be able to recall that information at this moment, and be able to make the appropriate verbal response. On top of it all, the child must be motivated and interested in giving the right response. A hostile or negativistic attitude, fear of possible failure, or anxiety about the consequences of giving the right response would all lead to the same outcome as would not knowing the correct answer. Clearly, intelligence—in the sense of being smart in the head—is not the only thing being measured by questions of this nature.

Let us look at a question similar to one that appears on the Similarities subtest. The child is asked, "In what way are cigar and cigarette alike? How are they the same?" In addition to all the abilities, functions, and attitudes that were necessary in order to succeed with the Information item, the child must now also be able to think in terms of concepts, engage in a certain amount of abstract reasoning. This probably comes closer to what most people would view as intelligence than did the sheer memory for facts required by the earlier subtest. But something else enters the picture with items like the cigar-cigarette example. Is it likely that the child whose father smokes will be in a better position to answer this question than the child whose parents abstain from the use of tobacco? What about the child who comes from a home where smoking is considered sinful? What about the child from a home where the smoking of one parent is a constant source of friction and discord? Would the associations aroused by this question interfere with giving an adequate response and is that child thus less intelligent than the one who has no conflict around this topic?

The items on the Arithmetic subtest are word problems that must be solved mentally without recourse to paper and pencil. This requires that the child be able to "do arithmetic," holding auditory information in short-time memory and sustaining attention until the problem is solved. All this probably has something to do with intelligence, but what may be more important, the task presupposes that the child has had the opportunity to learn the necessary computational skill. In many instances this is at least as much a function of educational opportunities as of intellectual ability. No matter how bright the child, if he or she has attended a school where arithmetic is taught poorly, low scores on this subtest will mean something other than low intelligence. Here is a typical question: "If you buy 6 apples at 78¢ a dozen, how much change should you get back from 1 dollar?" The child has 45 seconds to answer this question. Here, for the first time then, is a subtest which introduces a time limit. A correct answer given after the time limit has expired fails to receive credit. Slow, careful, reflective, children who are unsure of themselves will clearly be at a disadvantage. Intelligence? It is also worth noting that of the 14 test items available on the Arithmetic subscale for children over age eight, nine involve money and three others deal with buying or selling. One cannot help wondering what influence this has on the responses of children who come from homes with little money or where financial matters are a source of conflict and anxiety.

The Vocabulary subtest would seem a fairly straightforward measure of intelligence. The size of a person's vocabulary has long been viewed as a reflection of intellectual ability and nearly all tests of intelligence include vocabulary items in one form or another. Being asked, "What does hammer mean?" taps the child's verbal resources, not only in terms of familiarity with the word and the object for which it stands, but also in terms of the ability to describe this object, using a different set of words. It is not enough to know what "hammer" means; one must also be able to communicate this knowledge to the examiner. Again, this depends on past experience in a verbal environment. The child who comes from a home where communication is predominantly in terms of monosyllables and gestures will be at a handicap. In addition, there are again test items that may arouse anxiety in some children because of their associations. Words having to do with stealing or wagering or sickness do not contribute to making an emotionally neutral test.

The fifth subtest of the Verbal Scale is called Comprehension. Here the child is asked questions designed to tap his or her store of knowledge about practical issues that most children would have encountered at one time or another in the course of living in their culture. To some extent this subtest is intended to evaluate the child's judgment and common sense. Here are some examples of the kinds of questions asked: "What is the thing to do if you have lost your way in the city?" "Why do we have to put a dime in a pay telephone in order to make a phone call?" "Why is leather often used to make shoes?" The answers to these questions require fairly complex verbal statements, reflecting some logical reasoning.

Like some of the other subtests, this one permits two levels of scoring. One point is earned for a simple, relatively primitive answer; two points are awarded for a more complex, more sophisticated answer. Being able to do well on this subtest depends less on prior exposure to formal educational experiences than do such subtests as Information, Arithmetic, and Vocabulary. A child who is "street wise" might score quite high on Comprehension, for it is possible to have figured out some of the reasons on one's own. Since such "figuring out" is largely a function of what we call intelligence, this subtest would seem to come closer than many others to tapping the essence of what we are after. Provided, of course, that the child has not only worked out the answers to these questions but is also able to put these answers into words—and here we are back on the issue of different opportunities to acquire verbal communication skills, opportunities less available to the "street wise" than to the formally educated.

The sixth and supplementary verbal subtest is Digit Span. Here the child is asked to repeat from memory series of digits which the examiner enunciates at the rate of one per second. As on all the other subtests, the items are arranged in order of difficulty. A three-digit item (5-7-4) is used first, followed by a four-digit item, and so on, up to a seven-digit item which few children reach because the test is discontinued after two consecutive failures on a set of a given length. Following the presentation of the digits to be repeated as said by the examiner, the child is asked to listen to a new series of digits and to repeat each of these in reverse order. Here then, is a test that assesses a child's rote memory and ability to reproduce a sequential order. It is highly dependent on the ability to sustain attention and is thus easily disrupted by distractibility and lack of concentration. Anxious children, distractible children, or children with a short attention span will have trouble with this test. The kind of ability needed for doing well on this subtest is quite different from that called for by the other parts of the scale. Memory undoubtedly has something to do with intelligence, but echoing some numbers, even in reverse order, does not seem to require very highly developed mental processes. It is thus not surprising that this subtest has least in common with the other subtests in the entire Verbal Scale when their communality is evaluated by statistical means. Its correlation with other subtests is lower than that of all others with any other or with the overall test score. For this reason, Digit Span is not a part of the regular scale but a supplement used at the examiner's option.

The Performance Scale. This scale also contains five subtests plus one supplementary test. They are entitled Picture Completion, Picture Arrangement, Block Design, Object Assembly, and Coding. For the last subtest, a test called Mazes may be substituted. However, when it is not used as a subtest, Mazes serves as a supplementary test, analogous to Digit Span on the Verbal Scale.

It can be recognized that the word *performance* in the name of this scale is rather arbitrary since performance is required as much on the items of the verbal subtests as on the items described below. Equally arbitrary is the inclusion of the Picture Completion subtest in this second half of the WISC-R. All but this subtest require physical manipulation of test materials on the part of the child. Picture Completion calls for looking at a line drawing and telling what part of it is missing. Why this is not considered a verbal test is difficult to understand. The only way in which it differs from verbal subtests is in the fact that here the stimulus material is presented through the visual instead of the auditory mode. At any rate, the kind of pictures being shown are a clock with one of the numerals missing, a door with a hinge missing, or a person with an ear missing. (These are descriptions of actual items, there being little danger that this revelation will invalidate the test as might have been the case had we reproduced actual items from the Verbal Scale.) Aside from hearing and comprehending the instructions and knowing the meaning of the word "missing," the child will have to be able to tell essential from unessential detail. (The picture of the person's head has not only the ear but also the rest of the body missing, but only a reference to the ear earns a score!) In addition, the child will have to be able to focus attention on the aspect of the picture he or she has recognized as essential. Beyond these important intellectual capacities, the subtest requires relatively little. The pictures are all of objects that are so common that almost any child would be familiar with them. In addition, if a child does not know the word describing the missing part, pointing to the place where something is missing is an acceptable form of response. Despite its simplicity, this subtest is a fairly good way of assessing a child's intelligence and it serves to give one a sense of what intelligence is all about.

Picture Arrangement is a far more complex subtest which requires a number of different abilities if a child is to obtain a high score. Here the child's task is to arrange in logical sequence a series of from three to five pictures which, in their correct sequence, tell a simple story. There is, for example, a four-step illustration of a person who is oversleeping. The time shown on the alarm clock and his being in or out of bed provide clues to the correct sequence. The pictures are presented out of sequence and the child can earn points not only for the correctness of the arrangement but also for the speed with which the solution is presented. Many capacities must be called into play if a child is to earn a high score on this subtest. Details in the pictures must be discriminated, the situation must be understood, the temporal sequence of events depicted must be correctly recognized, the arrangement must be correctly recognized, and the arrangement must be accomplished in minimal time. In addition, there is a need for what might be called social intelligence in that the child must know the relationship between time and the act of getting out of bed—in the case of the item called "Sleeper"—or he must know the implications of having a man who wears a mask crawl through a window and being apprehended by a police officer. It should also be noted that the act of visual recognition and ordering of items in a sequential fashion involves the ability to perform a visual sequencing task. In some respects, this ability is related to an important requirement in reading where difficulties in visual sequencing are sometimes found in connection with reading disabilities. A child with such a reading disability might thus perform poorly on the Picture Arrangement subtest, not because of "low intelligence" but because the same problem that interferes with his or her reading is also disrupting the intelligence test performance.

The next item on the Performance Scale of the WISC-R is a task that has been a favorite with the designers of intelligence tests for many years. It is Block Design and calls for the visual analysis of a complex pattern and a subsequent synthesis of this pattern, using colored cubes. The child is shown a square, two-dimensional pattern composed of two colors, red and white. Four cubes painted either red or white, or red and white divided diagonally on their various sides, are placed on the table in front of the child. The instructions are to reproduce the pattern, using these cubes. Again there is a premium on doing this quickly, and the child who succeeds with the four-block items is also tested with larger designs requiring nine blocks for the solution. This task demands a nonverbal process of abstract reasoning inasmuch as the child must be able to visualize the component blocks within the total design and then succeed in reproducing this design from the three-dimensional objects. This is a complex mental operation, and as a result, this subtest is very sensitive to disruption by such factors as distractibility, anxiety, and problems with attention. In addition, many psychologists view good performance on this test as requiring an intact brain so that, conversely, poor performance is sometimes considered as a suggestion of the presence of a brain disorder. It should be obvious that poor block design performance is not an unequivocal sign of brain damage since poor performance can also be brought about by such psychological factors as anxiety or attentional problems.

The subtest called Object Assembly has some of the same characteristics as Block Design except that where the latter calls for the assembly of meaningless geometric designs, Object Assembly requires the child to put together cut up representations of a horse, a face, a car, and so forth. More than any other test in this series, this puzzlelike problem is similar to an activity the child will usually have encountered in other situations. Children who have had opportunities to play with jigsaw puzzles of varying degrees of difficulty will thus have an advantage over those who have been deprived of this common childhood activity. One might point out in this connection that block design toys, similar to the subtest we have just discussed, are also available in some of the better (and more expensive) toy stores. As on all other tests of intelligence and the tasks of which these are composed, the child with a comfortable and varied background will have the advantage over the one whose past experiences were in an impoverished surrounding. In the final analysis, an intelligence test is a test of how much of what a child has learned in the past he or she is able to put to use in the specialized situation represented by the intelligence test. The next and last subtest to be discussed may, in some respects, be an exception to this, for it tests not so much how much a child has learned in the past as how well he or she can learn *now*.

The subtest is called Coding. The child is shown a number-symbol code where a circle, for example, may stand for the numeral three, a cross for seven, and so forth from one to nine. In addition to this code, the working of which is demonstrated to the child, there is presented a sheet with rows of numbers under each of which there is an empty space. The child is instructed to draw into these spaces the appropriate symbol for each of the numbers. The score is based on both speed and accuracy. This task can be accomplished, of course, by looking at the number, checking the code sheet for the relevant symbol, and writing that symbol into the space before repeating this process for the next number. This slow and ponderous procedure would not earn a particularly high score. In fact, the time limit of 2 minutes might well have expired before the child got

very far with this approach. The more efficient way of accomplishing this task is quickly to learn the various numeral-sym-
bol combinations so that the checking of the code sheet can be
eliminated as soon as possible. This then tests the child's ability
to learn something new. Rote in nature and short-term to be
sure, but new learning nonetheless. Since one of the major uses
of intelligence tests is to predict how well a child should be able
to do in school, it is a shame that not more parts of these tests
assess a child's learning ability. The fact that the Coding subtest
measures a dimension of intelligence that is different from
those tapped by the other subtests is reflected in the statistic
which shows that the score on Coding bears less relationship to
the overall score of the WISC-R than any of the other subtests,
less even than Digit Span, about which we made a similar
statement.

The IQ Scores. We have presented a rather detailed discussion of eleven subtests of the WISC-R (the twelfth, Mazes, was
omitted because it is usually not given). The purpose of this
presentation was to communicate a feeling for what an intelligence test is all about since, as we have said, intelligence is
what intelligence tests test. The abilities that enter into the
performance on these subtests are thus what intelligence con-
sists of.

How is a child's performance on these tests put into the
shorthand form represented by the number we have come to
know by the term IQ? The first thing to remember is that the IQ
is no more and no less than a score that reflects a child's
performance on the test, expressed in a way that takes into
consideration his or her standing with respect to the "average
child" of that age. The norm for the average child is, of course,
based on the 200 children who served as representatives of that
age level when the test was first standardized.

How Fred Did on the WISC-R. Let us assume that nine-year-
old Freddie, whom we met in Chapter 1, had taken the WISC-R
and that his exact age at the time he took the test was 9 years
and 2 months. On the Information subtest Freddie gave nine
correct answers. His score, accordingly, was recorded as 9. The
average child of his age who participated in the original stan-

dardization of the test was able to obtain a score of 12. Freddie is thus below average. How much below average? To find the answer to this, one resorts to a statistical conversion of his score. The details of this need not concern us here, but the manipulation uses the convention of setting the number 10 as representing average performance and then expressing the individual child's achievement on a scale with respect to that norm. Converted into such a *scaled score,* Freddie's performance on Information would find expression in a scaled score of 7. Since the scaled scores for any subtest range from a low of 1 to a high of 19, with the average equal to 10, one can thus tell that Freddie's test performance on this subtest was below par. Available tables permit one to find out that Fred performed like a child of 7 years, 10 months, and that 84 percent of all children obtain higher scores than this. Freddie, in other words, is at the 16th percentile. Furthermore, had Freddie obtained the same score on all other subtests of the WISC-R, his IQ could be computed to be 85. But Information is only one subtest and one does not compute an IQ on that basis. All ten subtests must be considered before any meaningful conclusion can be drawn.

Let us look at another of the subtests, Object Assembly, and see how Freddie did there. He worked fast and accurately, accumulating a total of 24 points (out of a maximum score of 33 points). The average child of his age earns only 19 points, so Freddie did better than average on this subtest. Conversion of the points he earned into a scaled score gives us a score of 13. This is the level reached by the average child of 12 years and 10 months; Freddie is thus working some 3 years and 8 months above his age level when it comes to doing the kind of puzzles used in the Object Assembly subtest. What is more, had he worked at this level on all other subtests, his IQ would have been 115 and we can tell that only 15 percent of all children do better than this. That is, Freddie is at the 84th percentile in this particular performance.

Does the fairly large difference between the boy's performance on Information and on Object Assembly tell us anything? It tells us that this nine-year-old boy can perform almost as well as a thirteen-year-old when it comes to assembling puzzlelike representations of objects with his hands. On the other hand, when he is asked to give verbal responses to such questions as, "What does the heart do?" his answers are at the level of a child who is less than eight years old. Since the various subtests are scored in such a fashion that the average child obtains more or less the same scaled scores on all of them (that is the purpose of the scaling), we can say that Freddie is intellectually capable of performing considerably above his age level, that he has fairly high intelligence, but that something interfered with his ability to perform at that level on the Information subtest. What that "something" is becomes a matter of speculation, guesswork, and inference, and it is here that the psychologist's skill and experience in assessment comes into play.

Since little can be gained from comparing but two subtests, let us return to this question after a look at the table on page 78 in which Freddie's scores have been summarized. The column headings show the respective subtests and the rows reflect the various scores. The Raw Score is the number of points the boy earned. The Scaled Score is the conversion of these points into a number that makes the scores on the various subtests comparable in that the average is always set at ten. The row identified as Raw Norm shows the point-score an average child in the standardization group earned on each of the subtests. These can be compared with Freddie's Raw Scores to give an idea of how his absolute performance compared with what is expected of a child his age. Test Age, finally, is a conversion of Freddie's Raw Score into its equivalent in terms of years and months. It is the age of an average child who obtains a Raw Score at each of the respective levels. A Raw Score of 9 on Information, for example, is earned by an average child of seven years and ten months (here shown by the notation 7;10). The Raw Norm and Test Age are not computed in the ordinary use of this test. They are included here in hopes of aiding in the understanding of the meaning of intelligence test scores.

A look at Freddie's total performance reveals that he did better on the so-called performance tests than on the verbal tests. While the scores do not seem very far apart, an averaging of his Test Age equivalents tells us that on the Verbal Scale he functioned like an average child of nine years and seven months while on the Performance Scale he scored like a child of ten years and ten months. His low score on the Information test, which we

Intelligence Test Scores of a Boy Aged Nine Years, Two Months

	Info.	Simil.	Arith.	Vocab.	Comp.	Pic. Compl.	Pic. Arr.	B. Des.	Obj. A.	Coding
Raw	9	11	13	23	17	16	30	35	24	30
Scaled	7	10	14	9	12	9	13	14	13	8
Raw Norm	12	11	10	25–26	14	17	22	21	19	35
Test Age	7;10	9;2	11;6	8;2	10;6	8;6	12;10	12;6	12;10	8;2

Sum of Scaled Verbal Scores
52

Sum of Scaled Performance Scores
57

Average Verbal Test Age
9;7

Average Performance Test Age
10;10

Verbal Scale IQ
102

Performance Scale IQ
109

Full Scale IQ
105

commented on before, turns out to have been the lowest score on all subtests.

At this point we should remind ourselves of the fact that the Information test was the very first to be administered. Maybe a testing situation makes Freddie anxious; maybe new experiences are unsettling to him. But then we note that he also did rather poorly on the Vocabulary subtest which, in order of administration, is the seventh subtest presented to a child. Maybe the low score on Information was due to more than initial anxiety. Maybe Freddie has a somewhat limited vocabulary and a somewhat limited body of knowledge. But on Comprehension he did better than the average child his age, so his knowledge is not all that limited. What is?

The answer may lie in the fact that Vocabulary and Information call on knowledge usually acquired through school and by reading, while Comprehension knowledge is the sort of thing one can pick up in the course of everyday experience. Maybe what is reflected in this combination of test scores is the fact that Freddie is having trouble with school-related learning. But that seems to be limited to the area of reading since his score on the Arithmetic subtest is among his highest. Dealing with numbers or with relationships of objects in space does not give him trouble; his scores on Picture Arrangement, Block Design, and Object Assembly show this quite clearly. In fact, if one wanted to guess at Freddie's intellectual potential, these scores suggest that it may be close to that of the average twelve-and-a-half-year-old.

Is there something in the test performance that might permit us a guess about what it is that keeps Freddie from learning to read? The low Information and Vocabulary scores seem to be the consequences of his reading problem. What about the relatively low Picture Completion and Coding scores? These do not depend on reading. Coding, in fact, is best viewed as a test of ability to acquire new learning—new learning of a visual nature that entails a motor performance. Maybe Freddie has a problem in visual-motor coordination. But why the low Picture Completion score? No motor performance was required for that subtest. All he had to do was to look at the finer details of line drawings and to identify the missing parts. Looking at finer details and noticing minor discrepancies—that requires a focusing of attention, the ability to apply attention selectively. That—selective attention—is one of the most important capacities one needs to bring to bear in reading and in learning to read. Maybe Freddie's reading problem and the strange combination of subtest scores on his intelligence test have something to do with trouble in the area of selective attention. At least that is one inference we can draw. It is something to investigate further. Freddie is obviously not of low intelligence. His learning problem is not due to anything even resembling mental retardation; in fact, he is probably a child of superior intelligence who has a learning disability that may be related to problems in selective attention.

It should now be obvious that an intelligence test like the WISC-R gives the psychologist far more information than an IQ score. We have, in fact, postponed stating Freddie's IQ score until now because it is one of the least informative results which the intelligence test provides. As is well known, the average IQ of the total population is arbitrarily set at 100. Each individual's test performance can thus be expressed with respect to that theoretical average. Tables are provided by the test constructors which permit one to make the necessary conversion without engaging in complicated statistical computations. In Freddie's case, the sum of his Scaled Verbal Scores converts to a Verbal IQ of 102; the sum of his Scaled Performance Scores to a Performance IQ of 109. The combination of the two shows up in the relevant table as 105. This then is Freddie's Full Scale IQ. It is no more than a way of summarizing how he performed on the test items of which the WISC-R is composed. It tells us nothing of his "native intelligence," whatever that might be, and it tells us little about how well he ought to be doing in school. His test performance is far more a reflection of how much or how little he has learned thus far than it is a valid prediction of where he can go in the future. This must always be kept in mind when someone asks, "What's his IQ?"

The Illinois Test of Psycholinguistic Abilities (ITPA)

In continuing our attempt to answer the question which serves as the title of this chapter, "What can one tell from tests?," we turn next to an examination of what is the best known, most widely used test in the field of learning disabilities: the Illinois Test of Psycholinguistic Abilities.

Since a learning disability is a discrepancy between a child's potential for learning and his or her actual achievement, we should have a combination of tests which permits us to compare the child's potential and achievement. Intelligence tests, as we have seen, cannot assess potential with any degree of certainty. The ITPA, despite its popularity, was never meant to assess achievement, which is probably best assessed by what the child actually does in the classroom and by the kind of standardized achievement tests routinely used in most schools. What then, does the ITPA measure?

The revised edition of the ITPA was developed by Samuel and Winifred Kirk in collaboration with James McCarthy, *not* as a test for the classification of learning-disabled children, but as a device for assisting teachers wishing to help "cerebral palsied, brain-injured, and some emotionally disturbed children." As we said in an earlier chapter, Samuel Kirk came to the field of learning disabilities from work with the mentally retarded, and it had been there that his interest in so-called psycholinguistic abilities and disabilities first arose.

What is meant by *psycholinguistic?* The term was coined to denote the psychological aspects of language use and language acquisition. If you like, psycholinguistics deals with the things that go on in people's heads when they use language. Like other things that go on inside people's heads, one can study these functions only indirectly by observing what goes in and what comes out of the head and drawing inferences about what happens in between. To aid him in drawing these inferences, Kirk turned to a now rather outmoded theoretical model of communication which has three dimensions: channels of communication, levels of organization, and psycholinguistic processes. Since the ITPA was designed to assess functions in each of these three dimensions, it is well to examine these briefly so that we may understand the logic that underlies this rather complicated test.

Channels of Communication. This dimension deals with the means by which a message comes to the person and the way in which the person responds. What are the sense organs through which the message is received and what are the motoric means through which the message is delivered? The input may be visual, auditory, tactual, olfactory, or (to complete the list) gustatory. The output may take the form of vocal responses or any of a variety of muscular movements, such as pointing, nodding, grimacing, or foot stomping. If one is interested in language, one is primarily concerned about the receptive processes involving visual and auditory stimuli and the expressive processes involving verbal and manual responses. There are, of course, a variety of combinations of input and output, such as auditory-motor (hear and do), visual-vocal (see and say), and tactile-vocal (touch and describe), but the ITPA was designed to test only the auditory-vocal and visual-manual combinations. The omission of an assessment of the visual-vocal (see and say) combination is rather glaring, considering the fact that this is the channel that is involved in reading. Had this test been designed for use with learning-disabled children, it is very likely that the visual-vocal channel would have been considered. Its omission is a reflection of the original purpose of the test, to find a way of exploring the communication problems of mentally retarded children with whom reading is not a particularly pressing issue.

Levels of Organization. Here the model reflects the assumption that communication involves two levels of complexity. The first, the Automatic level, is fairly concrete. It would be operating in such activities as rote learning, simple repetitions, and well-established habits. The Representational level is where the more complex, abstract intellectual functions take place. These would include the grasping of meaning, the association of a symbol with the concept for which it stands, and the use of words to communicate ideas.

Psycholinguistic Processes. The use of language involves reception and expression at the input and output ends with an associational or organizing process between these points. In the theoretical model on which the ITPA is based, these processes are identified as the Receptive Process, the Organizing Process, and the Expressive Process. Reception involves obtaining meaning from the stimuli received, organization entails the manipulation of concepts, and expression calls for the ability to express ideas through words or gestures.

The combination of channels, levels, and processes forms a three-dimensional model in which each of the twelve subtests of the ITPA can be located. It is not necessary to be too concerned about the relevance of the tests to the model, which is more elegant in its theoretical construction than in its operational translation. Several of the functions identified in the model are not represented by tests. That is, the receptive and expressive processes at the automatic level are not examined in the administration of the ITPA. Thus, there is no way of testing the child's hearing and vision or his ability to make vocal sounds or motor movements as such. It has also been pointed out that some of the subtests are inappropriately placed or inaccurately labeled, probably because of the authors' attempt to fit the tests into the model, which may have become more of a procrustean bed than a device that furthers the advance of knowledge. However, be that as it may, a brief review of the nature of the various tests will provide an impression of the kinds of abilities that they require.

FUNCTIONS TESTED AT THE AUTOMATIC LEVEL

Closure. Here the ITPA assesses the child's ability to recognize objects when only partial clues to their presence are provided (visual closure) and to identify words when only some of the sounds making up a word are being said (auditory closure). A test of grammatic closure assesses the presumably automatic function required in giving the appropriate grammatic form of a well-known word. For example, the child is shown two pictures, one depicting one house, the other depicting two houses. The examiner says: "Here is a house; here are two _____" and the child is asked to fill in the missing word. Sound blending is another test in this array of tasks. Here the examiner pronounces the several sounds making up a word with half-second intervals interposed between the sounds, and the child is asked to tell what the word is (d – og = dog).

Sequential Memory. Two tests, one visual, the other auditory, evaluate the child's ability to reproduce a sequence of stimuli in their correct order. Auditory sequential memory is tested by asking the child to reproduce from memory a series of digits as soon as the examiner has finished saying them. To test visual sequential memory, the examiner presents the child with a series of simple designs and asks that this series be reproduced from memory by arranging plastic chips which bear these designs in the same order.

FUNCTIONS TESTED AT THE REPRESENTATIONAL LEVEL
At this level the symmetry of the model is more clearly preserved, for there are individual tests for the receptive, organizing, and expressive processes using both auditory and visual stimuli and vocal and motor responses.

Receptive Process. Here the goal is to test the child's ability to comprehend visual and auditory symbols. In the visual modality, the child is briefly shown a picture of, say, a running boy and asked, "See this?" There follows the presentation of a page containing four pictures: a standing girl, two seated girls, and a running girl. The child is now instructed to "find one here" and to point to the correct choice. To perform this task, the child must be able to abstract the idea of running and to use it in order to form the association between the running boy and the running girl. It should be obvious that this entails considerably more than mere "visual reception," which is an example of the rather misleading labeling of some of the subtests.

Auditory reception is tested by the presentations of such questions as "Do cats fly?" and "Do trees grow?" where the child is asked to give simple yes or no answers. This is thus a test of the child's ability to derive meaning from auditory stimuli and requires knowledge of words that become increasingly more difficult, plus an understanding of concepts that similarly range from very simple to highly complex. (One of the questions at the end of this subtest is, "Do migratory birds traverse?") Like all the other subtests, this one extends over a range of difficulty and the examiner stops presenting items when the child's performance shows that the limit of his or her ability has been reached.

Organizing Process. The tests designed to assess the child's ability to recognize the relationship between symbols and to organize and manipulate them, again use the auditory and the visual modalities. The tests are labeled Auditory Association and Visual Association. In the former, verbal analogies are presented to the child, who is expected to complete such sentences as, "Bread is to eat; milk is to _____." Because the emphasis of this test is on the child's ability to organize and associate concepts, the demands for receptive and expressive processes are minimal. The same holds true for the Visual Association test. Here the child is shown a picture of a table, surrounded by pictures of a horse, a mouse, an automobile, and a chair. The question "What goes with this?" is asked, accompanied by a pointing to the table, and the child is expected to point to the correct alternative, the chair in the present example. Again, as usual, the complexity of the task increases gradually until, at the most difficult level, visual analogies based on the relationship of geometric designs come to be used.

Expressive Process. The remaining two subtests are intended to assess the child's ability to use verbal or manual symbols in the expression of an idea. Verbal expression is elicited by showing the child an object, such as a pencil, with the request, "Tell me all about this." The score is based on the number of relevant facts the child can muster in describing and discussing the object. The test of manual expression is similar. Here the child is shown a picture of a common object, such as a spoon, with the request that he or she show the examiner what one does with it. The response is to be acted out in pantomime and the score is based on the number of appropriate gestures made by the child.

These tests obviously tap more than the ability to express ideas, for doing well on them requires that the child have had a variety of experiences under different conditions and that he or she possess a good memory and a vivid imagination. The visual recognition of the objects being presented and the comprehension of the examiner's request are, of course, further functions that enter into performance. There simply is no way of devising a test that isolates one and only one of the complex intellectual functions that enter into learning and communication. The originators of the ITPA cannot be faulted for having failed to do this; they can be taken to task for claiming to have developed an instrument that tests discrete abilities and can "pinpoint specific psycholinguistic abilities and disabilities."

What Can the ITPA Tell Us? What any test can tell us depends very largely on whether the instrument tests what it is supposed to test. This is known as the question of test validity. In the realm of mental functions, this question is extremely difficult to answer because it is so hard to define just what it is that we want the test to measure. A test of psycholinguistic ability presumably tests psycholinguistic ability. But what is psycholinguistic ability? And how can we find out whether a test like the ITPA does indeed measure that? As in the case of intelligence, the matter becomes very circular. We can say that psycholinguistic ability is what the Illinois Test of Psycholinguistic Ability tests and unsatisfactory as this is, it is really the best we can do. There simply is no external, independent criterion of psycholinguistic ability against which we could compare the ITPA in order to know whether it is valid. In the world of physical measures, the question of validity can always be answered by reference to some physical standard (which, when deposited in the Federal Bureau of Standards, is available for verification). In the world of psychological measures we have no absolute standards, and the question of test validity must often be resolved by asking whether the test is internally consistent, logically related to the construct it seeks to measure, and just simply "makes sense." Words like face validity, construct validity, and internal validity are often used, but they merely reflect that there is no such thing as criterion validity in psychological testing.

In the absence of criterion validity, a great deal depends on the adequacy of the normative group on whom the test was standardized. Although the ITPA was not intended to be a test for evaluating learning-disabled children, it is often used for this purpose. In that case, it becomes a test, not so much of psycholinguistic ability, as of learning ability and learning disability. Based, as it originally was, on a model of verbal communication, the ITPA has very little logical relationship to learning ability. None of the twelve subtests seek to measure learning, though adequate performance on many of them presupposes that learning has taken place in the past. Nor was the test standardized on learning-disabled children so that one might know what kind of performance one should expect from a child suspected of being learning disabled. The norms are based on the performances of 962 normally learning children between the ages of two years, four months and ten years, three months whose intelligence-test scores ranged from an IQ of 85 to an IQ of 115 with an average close to 100. It is with the performances of these children that one compares an individual child who has been given the ITPA.

As on intelligence tests, the raw scores which reflect the child's actual performance are converted into scaled scores which permit comparison of the performance on the different subtests as well as comparisons between children of different ages. Average performance on any one subtest is arbitrarily set at a score of 36. Eighty percent of the average children in the normative group scored within plus and minus six points from that mean. Any score within that range is thus considered "normal." A borderline discrepancy is any score that deviates more than six but less than ten points from a child's own mean; while a difference between the child's mean and a subtest score that is ten or greater is viewed as a substantial discrepancy, and, if in the negative direction, it is deemed indicative of a possible deficit. (For the statistically minded, a deviation of ten is more than 1½ standard deviation from the mean.)

The developers of the ITPA stress repeatedly that their tests should not be viewed as an instrument for classification, and while they speak of a Psycholinguistic Age which, as a summary score, reflects a child's overall performance, they would prefer if one looked only at the relationship among the various subtests in terms of the child's age and intelligence. In that fashion, the test becomes not an instrument that tells one what label to put on a child, but a device that gives one clue as to the steps to take to help a child through the remediation of deficits in the various functions the test seeks to assess.

The ITPA Scores of Fred. The nine-year-old learning-disabled boy whose IQ scores we discussed in connection with examining the WISC-R was also given the ITPA. His scores on the various subtests are shown in the form of a graph on the right side of Figure 1, under the heading "ITPA Scores." His

Figure 1
The ITPA Scores of Fred, aged 9 years, 2 months

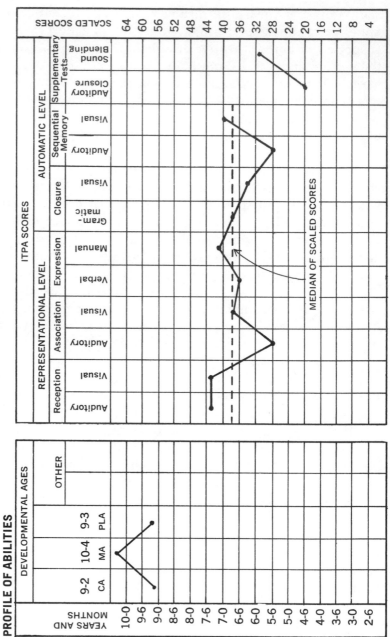

raw scores have been converted into scaled scores in order to make them comparable. The median of these scaled scores, 38, is indicated by the dashed line. (This measure is computed without considering the scores from Auditory Closure and Sound Blending, two "supplementary" tests, which had not been a part of the ITPA when it was originally standardized.)

If we use the rule of thumb that a deviation of ten or more points below the mean (or median) reflects a discrepancy in the function measured by that subtest, Freddie seems to be having trouble with Auditory Association, Auditory Sequential Memory, and Auditory Closure. In addition, his performance on the Sound Blending items was of borderline quality. The various scores can be combined into a Composite Score which is expressed in the form of years and months, thus permitting a rough comparison with a child's chronological and mental ages. For Fred, who is nine years, two months old, this composite score turns out to be nine years, three months. These relationships are shown in the graph on the left side of Figure 1, under the heading "Developmental Ages." What can we conclude from all this?

Though we know from his school performance that he is experiencing difficulty in learning to read, Fred's performance on tests involving the visual modality appears unimpaired. In fact, his adequacy in performing on these subtests places his overall performance, as reflected by the Composite Score, well within an age-appropriate, normal limit. On the other hand, on all but two of the tests involving the auditory modality, his performance is shown to be below par. The exceptions are Auditory Reception and Grammatic Closure. It thus appears that when Fred is asked questions like "Do trees grow?," which call only for yes or no answers, or when he is required to furnish a grammatic structure in completing such sentences as "Here is a house; here are two _____" (aided by a visually presented stimulus), Freddie experiences no difficulty.

Among other things, this tells us that there is nothing wrong with Fred's hearing; if that were the case, one would expect problems on all subtests involving auditory reception. He seems to be having trouble listening to a verbal message and processing it in terms of its meaning ("Bread is to eat; milk is to _____"), keeping something he just heard (a series of digits) in memory for a short time, hearing parts of a word and filling in the rest, and—to a somewhat lesser extent—blending sounds he has just heard into the whole word (d – og = dog).

The ITPA cannot tell us why Freddie has trouble with these tasks, but one can speculate that attending to auditory stimuli is a problem for him. Inasmuch as the teaching of reading places much emphasis on the auditory modality (the teacher pro-nounces words and models sound blending), his trouble in learning to read by this method might be based on this prob-lem. Those who rely on the ITPA for the evaluation of children with learning disabilities would now propose that Freddie be enrolled in a remedial program involving special exercises in sound blending, auditory memory, auditory closure, and audi-tory association in hopes of improving his performance in the areas of weakness. Here lies a potential pitfall.

It can be demonstrated that special exercises like those just mentioned will indeed improve a child's performance on the ITPA. Unfortunately, no one has ever demonstrated that such exercises will also improve a child's reading *unless* the exercises are accompanied by special remedial efforts in reading itself. It is also the case, however, that special remedial reading pro-grams can improve reading performance in the absence of training aimed at the so-called psycholinguistic functions.

All too often, tests like the ITPA take on a compartmental-ized autonomy whereby poor test performance leads to special-ized efforts whose goal is to improve test performance. Once that goal is reached, some people are very pleased with them-selves even though the problem (poor reading) that originally led to the administration of the test still exists unchanged. Properly used, the ITPA can be of help because it provides suggestions for methods of teaching reading that are likely to be more successful than others. In Freddie's case, a remedial read-ing program that limits demands on the auditory modality and emphasizes visual channels should probably work better than one which continues the heavy emphasis on the auditory chan-nel which characterizes the usual methods of instruction. Whether a good teacher needs a test to discover that a child learns better when taught by one method rather than another is an interesting question. At any rate, the ITPA is not a test that can be used to identify a learning-disabled child, nor do the special training procedures that focus specifically on the deficiencies which the test can identify do any more than improve ITPA test performance. They do not improve the child's learning of academic subject matter. Only the teaching of academic subject matter can do that. The test does provide clues, however, as to how such academic subject matter might best be taught, and in that way it can be a helpful tool for those who try to help a learning-disabled child.

The Marianne Frostig Developmental Test of Visual Perception

Before leaving the topic of what one can tell from tests, one more highly popular instrument that is frequently used with learning-disabled children should receive brief mention. It is the Developmental Test of Visual Perception (DTVP) originated by Marianne Frostig, whose name it bears. As the name of the test implies, the primary focus here is on visual perception, and it reflects the assumption that the learning problems of children are related to the level of the development in that area. The test thus seeks to assess this development in five supposedly independent abilities. Frostig provides a closely related training program that is designed to remediate any deficiencies that the test might uncover.

Again, as with the ITPA, we are thus faced with the question whether a learning-disabled child who is given the DTVP followed by specific training aimed at improving DTVP performance ends up being able to do better academic work. The answer, from available research, is "no." A group of reading-disabled children with "visual-perceptual difficulties" identified on the Frostig test were given 16 weeks of daily training, using the Frostig-Horne Program in Visual Perception (developed at the Marianne Frostig Center of Educational Therapy in Los Angeles). During that period a control group received the same amount of teacher attention. At the end, there was no difference in reading achievement between the group who had received the Frostig training and the group that had been the control.

It stands to reason that there is more to learning, whether it be reading or arithmetic, than eye-hand coordination, differentiation between figure and background, recognition of form constancy, positions in space, and spatial relations—the five areas tested by Frostig's instrument. Despite the best efforts of such leading figures in the field as Kirk and Frostig, we still do not have a test that will identify the learning-disabled child or really tell us what to do for such a child once he or she is recognized by various means.

THREE YEARS IN LIMBO—PART II

By the time Mary Jane was seen at the child guidance clinic in the city, she had been in the same "opportunity" class with the same teacher for more than three years. What had brought her to the clinic was the fact that a young pediatrician, who treated her for an ear infection, had been puzzled by her strange behavior which combined mannerisms often seen in blind children with those exhibited by the autistic, though, clearly, she was neither autistic nor blind.

The clinic to which the pediatrician had referred the Bronkowskys was staffed by child psychiatrists, clinical psychologists, reading specialists, and social workers. These professional people began a thorough study of Mary Jane. It extended over four weeks and included interviews with the parents, detailed psychological testing of the child, a visit to the child's school, and several meetings with Mary Jane for play interviews and diagnostic teaching aimed at trying to assess under what conditions the girl might be able to learn. When all of this information had been assembled and presented to a meeting of the professional staff, they concluded that Mary Jane had been grossly misclassified. Instead of being of borderline intelligence, she was probably, at least, a bright normal child, even though her overall intelligence test score was currently in the mental deficiency range. Considering the education she had not been receiving during the past three years, this was hardly surprising.

In all likelihood, Mary Jane had been perceptually immature when she had first been expected to do prereading exercises and had not been ready to do the work required of her in kindergarten. The ill-advised, unfortunate attempt to use tests administered by untrained hands in hopes of understanding her difficulty had served as a self-fulfilling prophecy. Being called "borderline," Mary Jane had been treated as such. She had been placed in an understaffed and underfinanced parody of a special education class where, not being expected to learn, she failed to learn. Except that she learned one thing; to imitate the behavior and mannerisms of some of her blind, retarded, autistic, and brain-injured classmates who, as she must have been quick to notice, received much teacher attention for these mannerisms.

After a year or so of intensive therapeutic and remedial work at the clinic and placement in a special school for learning-disabled children, Mary Jane made remarkable progress. Her family moved into the city where she eventually entered regular public school and did satisfactory work only one grade behind her age-appropriate placement.

Another cheering ending to this otherwise dismal tale is that the state in which this took place amended its education laws so that all children, regardless of their special needs, must be provided with an *appropriate* education. With state support, children in local school systems can now have access to evaluations by trained professional people and receive whatever special schooling their particular handicaps, disabilities, or developmental conditions demand. Future Mary Janes should not have to mark time in schoolrooms which are no more than repositories for children who are too much trouble for the teachers in regular classrooms. The improvements in conditions in this state and others is largely due to the efforts of such organizations as the Association for Children with Learning Disabilities, the American Association on Mental Deficiency, and the Council for Exceptional Children, to whom all who care about children must be deeply indebted.

Chapter 6

WHAT HAVE WE LEARNED FROM RESEARCH?

Many of us share a faith that most if not all our questions about the world in which we live will ultimately be answered through the application of the scientific method. Research has enabled mankind to solve many problems; research should be able to solve the problem posed by the learning-disabled child. This faith in science is well founded, no doubt, but one must recognize that the results of research are not quickly obtained. It takes years, decades, centuries to move from ignorance to knowledge, and there are many false leads that must be followed, errors that must be rejected, disappointments that must be borne before a problem is fully solved. Considering the fact that research on learning disabilities began no more than ten years ago, it is not surprising that we are far from having definitive answers to our questions.

Before one can hope to do meaningful research on a problem, the problem must be recognized and its area circumscribed. The recognition of the problem we have come to call learning disabilities is very recent and even now, not all agree that there is such a problem. Even those who have come to use the term (thus presumably recognizing the existence of the problem) so far fail to agree which children should be included, which excluded from the category. Until such agreement is obtained, research will be conducted on mixed groups of children and useful results will be unlikely to come forth.

At least as vital as agreement on the existence of a problem, and on a limiting definition that circumscribes the area to be studied, is the formulation one uses to guide one's research. We have already touched on the implications of viewing learning-disabled children as brain-damaged. If one formulates the problem in this manner, one is likely to seek confirmation of the brain-damage hypothesis, and years of research have been necessary in order to disprove that notion. If one formulates the problem of learning-disabled children as synonymous with hyperactivity, one selects hyperactive children and the focus of one's studies then becomes their motor activity—not their difficulty in learning. Assumptions about language problems, visual development, neurological impairment, or memory disorder have all resulted in studies which were aimed roughly in the direction of solving the puzzle presented by learning disabilities. None have provided an answer.

We are still at the beginning of what may be a long search for the key to Freddie's problem. The research scientist is used to taking the long view of things. Many small research results, carefully and imaginatively strung together, should eventually make sense and reveal answers to such questions as what to do for the learning-disabled child and how to prevent future children from thus becoming disabled. That, clearly, is not very satisfactory for Freddie and his parents. They need answers now; twenty or more years from now, answers won't do them much good.

The clinically oriented research scientist is all too familiar with that dilemma. Answers are needed now but research won't provide them until much later. Freddie can't wait; what can we do? Some have called this problem "the clinical bind," the problem of needing answers while knowing that the final answers are not available. It is important that we admit that we don't know the answer; only in that way will we continue to search for it. At the same time, we must do the best we can for children who need help now so that the recommendations we make for Freddie and all the other learning-disabled children are based on the knowledge that is presently the best we have available. It is with that goal, to present the best available current knowledge, that the following lines are written.

Selective Attention

When a child has trouble copying a pattern on a marble board, or is unable to repeat a rhythmic series of taps, or can't find pictures hidden in a diffuse background, what is the basis of that difficulty? To say that this child has a perceptual-motor problem, or a visual-motor problem, or a sequencing problem, or a figure-ground problem is saying little more than what has already been observed. It is giving the observation a more or less fancy descriptive label. Learning-disabled children have been found to have one or the other (and sometimes all) of these difficulties, yet knowing that has helped us—and the children—very little. Is there some function which is required by all of these tasks, a function which, were it to be deficient, would explain why a child experiences difficulty on these tasks? At this point, the best candidate for nomination as such a function is selective attention. As we shall see, this function is essential for good performance on marble boards, tapping tests, hidden-pictures tests, and many other tasks on which learning-disabled children encounter difficulty—to say nothing of learning to read or to do arithmetic.

What Is Selective Attention? The word "attention" has many meanings and, not unlike learning, it is one of those words where we think we all know what they mean only to find, on a moment's reflection, that its definition is not at all obvious. When a teacher notices that a student is looking out of the window, that teacher may say, "Jimmy, pay attention!" Actually, Jimmy is probably paying attention (to the airplane in the sky), but he is not paying attention to whatever it may be that the teacher wants him to attend to at that moment. Now suppose that, upon the teacher's appeal, Jimmy directs his glance at teacher or chalkboard. The teacher may now be satisfied that Jimmy is "paying attention"—but is he? How can the teacher tell whether the child is paying attention? Certainly not from the direction of the child's glance, for we all know that we can look at something without seeing it, hear something without listening to it. Attention is more than receiving sensory stimulation; attention involves what we do with the stimuli to which we are exposed. It is, in other words, an internal, so-called cognitive process. As such, the only way another person can seek to tell whether a child is "paying attention" is to ask a question that can only be answered if the child has been attentive. The teacher may do this by asking, "Jimmy tell me what I just said," although the child's answer to that is also no guaranteed indication of whether or not Jimmy had been attending.

Suppose the child is able to echo the teacher's last sentence; is that really proof of attention? Or suppose the child can't repeat what the teacher said; is that proof of lack of attention? Could it be that the child attended but did not understand? Could it be that the child attended but can't remember? Could it be that the child is not motivated to answer the teacher's question because the reprimand annoyed him? As in the case of learning, the only way we can tell whether attention is present is by drawing inferences from a child's performance and these inferences are often of questionable validity.

What we call attention has two major aspects. One has to do with how much attention a person is devoting to a given aspect of the world around him. When listening to music, for example, one can concentrate on it very intently or one can let it serve as background while attending to other matters. "Hovering attention" would describe this latter condition. Another aspect of attention has to do with the fact that we can focus our attention on various parts of the available stimulation. In listening to music, again, one can focus one's attention on the words of a song, on the part played by the flute, on the rhythm, on the melody, or on the overall impression made by the composite. This partly intentional and voluntary focusing of attention on an aspect of the stimulus field is what has been designated *selective attention.*

SELECTIVE ATTENTION AND LEARNING

At any given moment a person receives stimuli from a great many sources and through every sense receptor. Visual, auditory, and tactile nerve fibers are carrying messages from the environment, while other nerves, called kinesthetic and proprioceptive, bring messages from inside our own body. These many messages often call for conflicting and mutually incompatible responses. Behavioral chaos would result if we were not equipped with the capacity to *select* among these nerve impulses and to *attend,* and thus to respond, to one or a limited number of them at a time. Selective attention is thus a highly adaptive capacity, and any difficulty in the use of this capacity would clearly represent a considerable handicap. This is particularly true in any situation where one is required to learn something.

In even the simplest learning situation, a person is exposed to a complex mixture of stimuli but the response is to be learned to only one aspect of this combination. Take, for example, a child who is supposed to learn to say the sound *bee* to the visual presentation of the letter *b* written on a chalkboard. Among the stimuli being received by this child at that moment is not solely the shape of the letter but also the teacher's pointing finger, the teacher's voice saying the sound, the buzzing of a fly in the room, other things written on the board, the color of the board, the color and size of the letter, a pinching shoe, a growling stomach, the pressure of the seat, a random thought, and so forth. The child is looking at what the teacher is pointing to, he is "paying attention," but unless he is selectively attending to the shape of the letter and the sound made by the teacher's voice, he is not going to learn reading the letter *b*. Thus, before any learning can take place, the child must have developed the capacity to use selective attention. If selective attention is not functioning properly, the child will have trouble learning.

Such trouble can, of course, take many forms. Should the child attend only to the teacher's voice and not also to the written letter, the teacher would hear the child say, "bee" and assume that the pupil is learning to read. The error of this assumption will emerge only later when, in the absence of the teacher's voice, the letter alone fails to get the child to make the correct response. Attending only to one part of a stimulus combination might be termed *overexclusive attention* and, as we shall see later on, it is probably an immature way of attending to one's environment.

It is also conceivable that a child overexclusively attends only to the circular portion of the letter *b*. At later testing, this child would say the sound *bee* when shown the letter *d* because it also has a circular portion. One would thus observe the *b-d* reversal that is so frequently displayed by beginning or poor readers. Another child might attend to the teacher's pointing finger and the sound of the teacher's voice but not to the symbol which is indicated by the finger. This child would learn to vocalize "bee" to the sight of a teacher's pointing finger, no matter what the target of the pointing. Or a child might be attending to the buzzing fly and learn to call it "bee." Yet another child with problems in selective attention might attend not only to the distinctive features of the sound and letter which are central to the task at hand, but also to the color of the chalkboard and the pointing finger. Such overinclusive attention might result in the child being able to produce the correct answer only when the same combination of stimuli is again presented. That is, written on a different surface or not indicated by a pointing finger, the letter *b* would not evoke the word *bee*.

Immature or inadequate use of selective attention can thus result in a variety of maladaptive behaviors when a learning task requires that the child focus on that aspect of the situation which those seeking to teach consider to be the distinctive features. We have a variety of words that are used to label children who show the maladaptive behaviors that can result from problems in selective attention. They may be called mentally retarded when they can't learn to associate the letter with the appropriate sound and simply echo the teacher's words. They may be called learning disabled if they confuse letters like *b* and *d*. They may be called psychotic if they say "bee" every time the teacher points to something, no matter what. They may be called autistic if they insist on calling flies "bee," or they may be deemed brain-damaged if they are so "rigid" as to be able to give the right answer only when the selfsame conditions as in the original learning situation are again present. In other words, problems with selective attention may be the basis of a variety of somewhat similar conditions.

Note, too, that descriptive terms like "distractible" and "hyperactive" may come into play as a result of a child's problem with selective attention. The child who attends to the fly instead of the letter on the chalkboard has selected what, from the teacher's point of view, is the "wrong" thing. The teacher may perceive this as the fly having distracted the child and call the child distractible. If, on the other hand, the child has selectively attended to the pressure of the seat on his back and responds to this (appropriately) by shifting position or standing up, the teacher notices that there is more activity than is deemed appropriate for this situation—hyperactivity.

If selective attention is the basis of learning disabilities and also of distractibility and hyperactivity, one can understand why so many learning-disabled children are described as distractible and hyperactive. The conclusion, drawn by some, that this points to brain damage would be valid only if problems with selective attention could be explained only on the basis of brain damage. This, as we shall soon show, is not the case.

SELECTIVE ATTENTION AND PERFORMANCE

Problems with selective attention can interfere not only with learning but also with the performance of what has been learned. Assume, for the moment, that a child has learned what sound the letter *b* symbolizes. This letter is now shown to the child together with the question, "What sound does this letter make?" The child's attention is supposed to be focused on this combination of visual and auditory stimuli. They are to what he should selectively attend. But what if the child attends instead to any of a dozen other stimuli that are also present at this moment and says, "It's the siren of a fire engine" or "My stomach is growling" or "My uncle has a new puppy" or "Tomorrow is Friday"? Each of these would be an appropriate response to a current stimulus, some external, some internal, but they result from a failure to attend to the stimulus the teacher considers "right" and the answers are therefore "wrong." Again terms like distractible, autistic, psychotic, or retarded may enter the picture but a new one now joins this list. It is "impulsive." From the teacher's point of view, the child seems to have blurted out the first thing "that came to his mind." That is, he said not what was in the teacher's mind, that to which the teacher was selectively attending, but that which was in the child's own mind, that to which he was selectively attending. It should not come as a surprise that impulsiveness is another characteristic often attributed to learning-disabled children.

None of this is meant to assert that what the child is attending to or how the child responds is "right" and that the teacher is "wrong" in expecting the child to give a response that is appropriate to the task at hand. Reality, after all, is what the majority of people in our society view as reality and the teacher in the classroom is a legitimate representative of that society. A child who fails to give the expected answer is wrong, no matter what the reason for the answer. We are not here trying to say that the child is right; we are merely trying to show how the child might have arrived at what the teacher correctly views as the wrong answer. For it is only if we can understand how children come to give wrong answers that we can learn to help these children to give the right answers, the answers expected by their society and without which living in this society would be well-nigh impossible. By understanding what it takes to give the right answers, we can stop such ineffective things as yelling at children to "pay attention," or punishing them for giving wrong answers, or writing them off as retarded, brain damaged, or psychotic.

Selective Attention and Learning Disabilities

Learning disabilities are due to problems in the area of selective attention, and the frequently reported distractibility, hyperactivity, and impulsiveness of learning-disabled children are the results and not the cause of their problem. This is an assertion that must now be backed up by referring to research on selective attention. This review of research will also lead us to the probable answer to the question of what it is that makes learning-disabled children have problems with selective attention. Beyond that, we shall arrive at some suggestions of what might be done to help learning-disabled children once one has decided that their problem is basically one of selective attention. That, after all, is the bottom line, the ultimate point of all theorizing and all research: How can it help my child?

Research on Selective Attention. Like all other processes we presume to be going on in the brain, selective attention can be studied only by indirect means. If one presents an individual with a task which can be solved only if one attends to it in a selective manner, and if one then observes that the individual solves the task correctly, one can conclude with a good degree of assurance that selective attention has been employed. What this entails is an inference about the occurrence of a process based on observations of a stimulus at the input end and a response at the output end. It is by such inferences that one seeks to validate a construct like selective attention.

Note that the inference is possible only when the person solved the task correctly. If one presents a stimulus and no response or a wrong response takes place, it is impossible to infer that selective attention was absent, because the failure to produce a correct response may have been due to a great many different reasons, other than (or in addition to) a failure in selective attention. The task may have been too difficult, the person may have been unable to remember an important fact, lack of motivation may have kept the person from performing, and so forth. As usual, a failure to find evidence for a phenomenon cannot be taken as proof that the phenomenon does not exist. Science can only prove, never disprove.

When one deals with a construct like selective attention, it is well to have different methods on which to base inferences about the construct. The more methods point to the operation of the construct, the more confidence we can have that our inferences are valid. It is a way of establishing what is known as *construct validity*. In the case of selective attention, five different research methods have been addressed to the issue. They are signal detection, dichotic listening, incidental learning, component selection, and the monitoring of heart rate changes. Let us take a brief look at each of these methods and summarize what has been found.

SIGNAL DETECTION

In this method, the child is asked to make a simple motor response, such as pressing a button, whenever a light or similar stimulus appears on a display. It is possible to increase the complexity of this task by requiring one response to one kind of stimulus, and another kind of response to a different stimulus, such as: Push the button on the left when the red light comes on and the button on the right when the bell rings. If several stimuli are presented simultaneously, where each controls a different and mutually exclusive response, it is possible to ascertain to which of the stimuli the child is selectively attending. Such an arrangement was used in a study in which the performances of normal and retarded readers were compared. It demonstrated that the retarded readers had great difficulty with the task, suggesting (but not proving) that these retarded readers had trouble in the area of attention.

DICHOTIC LISTENING

This is a variation on the method of signal detection. Here the child is given two different auditory messages which are delivered through earphones, one to the left, one to the right ear. In the simplest situation, the child is merely asked to report what he has heard or to answer questions that pertain only to the content of one of the two messages. At a somewhat more complex level, the child is instructed to listen only to the message coming in through one ear and to ignore what is heard on the other ear. Finally, it is possible to combine this with instructions also to listen for a specific signal (which arrives on the unattended ear) and to make a response, such as pressing a button, whenever that signal is detected. A child who is selectively attending to the channel to which he has been instructed to listen would miss many of the signals, while a child with more limited selective attention would pick up many of them. With such a method, children with reading problems have been found to experience difficulty and learning-disabled boys have been reported to be unable to attend only to the information from just one ear. Thus, this provides another hint that learning disabilities may have something to do with selective attention.

Two other interesting results have been obtained with dichotic listening tasks. One is that children's ability to perform on this task improves with age. The other is that performance can be improved if one provides systematic training that includes rewards for success. If selective attention is involved in this performance, this would suggest that poor selective attention is not an irreversible deficit, but rather a skill that changes over time and can be improved through training.

INCIDENTAL LEARNING

This method has been used more extensively than the others and it provides a nice illustration of what selective attention is all about. The basic model of these studies can be described by the following situation. A child is shown a stack of cards on each of which is a picture of an animal and a picture of a common household object. The child is instructed to sort these cards so that all the lions are in one pile, all the cows in another pile, and so forth. The instructions thus focus the child's attention on the animals and on the location of the respective species. This is known as the central task. The number of cards correctly sorted can be used as a score on the central task, the central score.

After the child has completed this sorting, however, the experimenter asks which household object went with the lions, which with the cows, and so on. The child had obviously not been instructed to attend to this association and anything he or she noticed about this would have been incidental to the central task. For this reason, this aspect of the procedure is called the incidental task and the number of associations correctly stated serves as the incidental score. The learning reflected by this score is incidental learning for, in addition to having dealt with the central task which required attending to the animals, the child has also—incidentally—acquired information about the accompanying household object. It is now possible to compare the central score with the incidental score. Their relative magnitude gives one a measure of the degree to which selective attention was operating. The higher the incidental score, the lower selective attention; the lower the incidental score, the higher selective attention.

Incidental learning and selective attention thus stand in inverse relationship to each other. The better a child is able to focus attention on the central task (as the instructions demanded), the less he or she will learn about the incidental features. Conversely, the more incidental matter was learned, the less attention is likely to have been paid to the central task. In a sense, high incidental learning goes along with an inefficient mode of processing information, for the more attention one pays to the unessential (from the point of view of the task at hand), the less attention one can devote to the essential. In reading, for example, the task demands that many incidental aspects of the stimulus situation, such as brightness and size of letters, be ignored and attention concentrated on the shape, order, and spacing of the letter combinations. A poor reader might be one who attends not only to the central but also the incidental aspects of the printed material and to other extraneous stimulation. In an incidental learning task, a poor reader might be expected to achieve high incidental and low central scores if the capacity to attend selectively were not functioning at an optimal level. Indeed, there are studies which show this to be the case. Compared to good readers, poor readers show more incidental learning; they have, presumably, less adequate selective attention.

Like other methods which reflect the operation of selective attention, incidental learning changes as children get older. From early childhood through adolescence the ability to attend selectively to the critical features of a stimulus and to ignore the unessential aspects undergoes gradual improvement. Beginning sometime in early adolescence and from that time until a decline with advanced age, a person is capable of turning attention selectively to that aspect of the environment which is central to the performance of a given task. In proofreading, for example, we are able to attend closely to the spelling of words, while ignoring their meaning and thus the content of what we are looking at. Yet when that task is completed, we are able to focus our attention on the content, and when we do, we often overlook spelling errors or even an omitted word.

COMPONENT SELECTION

When incidental learning is used to tap a child's attention, the experimenter arbitrarily designates which aspect of the task is central and which is incidental. When the child is told to sort the animals, the household objects are implicitly defined as incidental. This method cannot be used, therefore, to find out whether the child would, on his own, attend more to one aspect of the stimulus complex than to another or which of the aspects he would thus select. The method of component selection was designed to solve this problem. It taps the disposition of children to attend selectively to a single feature of a multifaceted stimulus by allowing free choice of the means by which to discriminate among stimuli.

Component selection studies involve two parts, a learning phase and a test phase. During the learning phase the child is asked to sort a series of cards into different piles. Each of these cards bears a different shape (circle, square, heart, star, etc.), and each shape is of a different color. Thus, the circle is always blue, the square always green, and so forth. The experimenter makes no mention of the two components of each stimulus (the shape and the color) but merely asks the child on which pile a given card is to go. The task can thus be accomplished by attending to either the shape or the color or to both, but since a premium is placed on doing it quickly, it is more efficient to ignore one of the components (since the two are redundant) and to attend only to either shape or color.

During the test phase it is possible to assess what approach the child had used for the sorting, whether shape or color had been selected as the component that served as the basis for categorizing the stimulus objects. This is done by showing the child each of the components by itself, such as an all blue card or a white circle on a black background. The child is asked to continue to indicate on which pile each of these cards is to be put, and the experimenter can thus ascertain whether the child had selected a component during the learning phase and, if so, which one. For example, a child who had originally sorted solely on the basis of shape would be able to do very well when shape alone is presented but very poorly when color alone is shown. The child's performance can now be expressed in terms of shape scores and color scores, permitting one to make comparisons among groups of children at different age levels.

When one compares four-, eight-, and twelve-year-olds on component selection tasks, one again finds a developmental trend. At the youngest age level the children seem to attend primarily to shape. This dimension appears to dominate their perception, leaving little room for self-directed selective attention. The expression *stimulus bound* has sometimes been used to describe this reaction of young children. With increasing age, there is increasing attention to color. By the age of eight, the color scores on component selection tasks are nearly as high as the shape scores. At this age children appear to attend to both components, using relatively little selective attention. It is not until age twelve that selective attention comes into play. At that age level, children seem to become more flexible in their attention deployment and they differentiate between conditions in which attending to several stimulus features can be useful and situations in which it is more efficient to exercise selective attention.

HEART RATE

The methods for studying attention we have discussed thus far all base the measures on a response which is made by the child, such as button pressing or card sorting. These approaches introduce a variety of variables that may have nothing to do with selective attention, such as motivation and cooperation with the experimenter. When the monitoring of a child's heart rate is used to indicate whether and to what the child is attending, these possible sources of error are eliminated.

It is known that heart rate slows down when a person anticipates the appearance of a signal, engages in visual fixation, or scans a stationary or moving object. Such slowing also takes place when the person is presented with a novel, surprising, changed, or new stimulus. Furthermore, changes in heart rate are related to reaction time and to accuracy of perceptual judgments, and since all these situations involve attentional processes, measures of heart rate changes have come to be used as an index of attention.

Using the recording of heart rate, it has been demonstrated that children who are referred to a clinic because of attentional and learning difficulties differ from a normal control group in that they show less heart rate deceleration while they are anticipating the appearance of a signal to which they have been asked to make a response. If one accepts the heart rate measure as related to attention, this would again suggest that learning-disabled children have a problem in the area of attention. Incidentally, when such children are given the drug Ritalin, their heart rate deceleration and reaction time increases significantly, suggesting that when such medication is effective, it may be so because it serves to improve a child's ability to focus attention.

BEHIND THE SCENES OF RESEARCH

By the time a research study is mentioned in a book, all that one usually reads there is a summary of the results and their implications. Even the original article that appeared in a scientific journal had essentially been a summary of the methods used, the results obtained, and the conclusion drawn. What is never reported are the trails and tribulations through which the researchers had to go before they could get to their finished product. Let us recount— again in summary form—some of the experiences we had in conducting one of the studies mentioned in this chapter.

We wanted to do a study comparing the performances of children with reading problems to those of good readers on a task that measures incidental learning. In addition, we were interested in finding out whether children's performance on this task changes as they get older. Therefore, we also wished to compare children from different age groups. The task is simple and children view it as a game. It involves no more than looking at some pictures and helping sort them into different piles according to their content. The whole activity takes about fifteen minutes. At the end each child, regardless of his or her performance, gets a small present to reward participation.

Let us skip the mechanical preparations of designing the study, deciding on the method to be used, and obtaining the pictures we needed for our work. Let us, instead, recount the administrative or, if you will, political steps through which we had to go before we could get to see the first of the 60 children we wished to test.

The initial step in this procedure was to obtain clearance from the Committee on Research Involving Human Subjects, a group of representatives from various departments at our university. This committee is required by federal regulations and exists to protect participants in research from potential abuses such as stress, pain, deception, dangerous drugs, or risky medical procedures. Since our little game entailed none of these, we thought that our written request for clearance would be given quick approval. Wrong. The committee wrote back, wanting to know how we were going to obtain the "informed consent" of the parents of children we wanted to take part in our study. As is usual when working with schoolchildren, we had intended to obtain parental permission, but we had failed to include in our proposal the details of the method by which this was to be done. We thus drew up a form letter that was to be sent to all participants' parents. The material was returned to the committee. After two weeks had passed without an answer, we inquired and found that one of the committee members had misplaced our request. A duplicate set was sent. And so it went. Six weeks after we had originally sought clearance, we finally received permission to proceed.

Next began our search for a school where we might find the children for our study. Through a personal friend who happened to be a reading specialist in a public school, we were introduced to his principal. Principals are busy people and it took us nearly two weeks to get an appointment with her. We explained what we were trying to do. She seemed interested, particularly when we pointed out that a study like ours might eventually lead to better ways of teaching children with reading problems. But no, she could not give us permission to go ahead. She first had to discuss the proposal with her superintendent who, in turn, had to clear it with his school board. A month went by before we got word that the project had been approved. Yet, because this elementary school did not have enough children with reading problems at the grade levels we wanted to study, we had to approach two additional principals. Now things went a little more quickly because the superintendent and school board had already given their approval.

Now we selected from the class roster the names of the children with whom we wished to work. Over the principals' signatures, we mailed the requests for permission to the children's parents. We had originally thought that we could simply ask parents to respond only if they objected and to assume that those from whom we did not hear had nothing against their child's participation. The committee on human subjects had rightly insisted on a positive reply. That is, before we could work with any given child we had to have a signed statement from his or her parents saying that they were giving their permission. Getting the children we needed for the study thus entailed follow-up notes and telephone calls to those who had not returned the permission slip. Another four weeks went by before this step was completed.

By now it was time for Christmas vacation. After that came a meeting with all teachers during which we explained to them what we intended to do. We agreed that we would work our schedule around events like quizzes, movies, class outings, and the like. Needless to say, when we got to set up sessions for specific children, some were out sick, others refused to leave their classroom, and a few could not understand our instructions. A couple of times our car broke down, a research assistant had to go home on a personal emergency, and a snowstorm closed both university and school for a couple of days.

Given all these hurdles and complications, we consider ourselves fortunate that we ever got to the point where we could score and analyze our results. The article in which we reported the study was published two-and-a-half years after we had begun. People sometimes wonder why there is so little research on the learning problems of children. The real wonder is that any research gets done at all!

What Does All of This Mean?

We have seen that different investigators who have approached the topic from diverse points of view and with a variety of different measures demonstrated the operation of selective attention. The idea that there is something like selective attention that operates when people process information seems rather sound. At the very least, the idea or construct is useful when one tries to understand why some children have difficulty in processing information, why they are learning disabled.

In addition, there is a theme that runs throughout these studies on selective attention. It is that selective attention improves as children get older. There are developmental changes that can be demonstrated with every one of the measures used to assess selective attention, be it heart rate deceleration, signal detection, dichotic listening, incidental learning, or component selection. Whenever normal children at different age levels were compared on these tasks, the younger did worse than the older and improvement in performance showed a regular increase with increasing age—up to early adolescence. What is more, the performance of learning-disabled children showed a striking similarity to the performance of younger, normal children. *This strongly suggests that learning disability represents a developmental lag in the acquisition of the ability to sustain selective attention.* This would mean that learning disability is not due to some abnormality in the brain but rather to individual differences in the rate at which children develop the ability to use selective attention, an ability that is crucial for certain kinds of learning.

The Development of Selective Attention. Any human capacity that undergoes developmental changes will reflect individual differences on at least two important dimensions. One dimension is the *rate* of development; some children reach a given point in development earlier, some later than others. We are familiar with this phenomenon from even casual observations of children's growth and development. It is obvious in the realm of physical growth and apparent in the development of such intellectual aspects as language.

The second dimension on which individual differences can be found is the *quality* of any given capacity that is available to a child. Whether one expresses this in terms of quantity, magnitude, or intensity, some children will be better, some worse in any particular facility; some will have more, some less of whatever it is we are assessing. Here, however, casual observation is not always sufficient, for the differences in quality may be subtle and may, therefore, call for sophisticated measurements, such as tests of intelligence.

We can demonstrate the operation of these two dimensions of development by referring to the simple motor behavior of running. We all know that some children can run earlier than others, though all physically normal children will eventually be able to run. At that point, however, some will be able to run faster than others, though to check this out, one may need to use a stopwatch in making comparisons. It is also true that with some training the slow runner can learn to increase his or her speed—up to a point. There are probably physical limits to how fast any given individual is able to run, no matter how intensive the training, though we won't know what that limit is unless we expose the person to training. This is the problem of assessing a person's potential which we discussed in an earlier chapter.

Individual differences in rate of development and quality of capacity attained have been found in every human ability ever studied. Thus, there is every reason to assume that one will also find individual differences in rate and quality if one examines the development of the capacity to sustain selective attention. Thus far, we have research evidence pointing to differences in *rate* of development; qualitative differences remain to be studied. What follows, therefore, is based only on the assumption that there are individual differences in the rate of development of selective attention. We want to explore how this fact might relate to the phenomenon of learning disabilities, but it should be stressed that this exploration is still in the realm of speculation.

OVEREXCLUSIVE ATTENTION
The very young child's attention can be said to be "captured" by one aspect of the stimulus field, and the infant attends to that to the exclusion of all other aspects, some for longer, some for shorter periods of time. Furthermore, some infants consistently orient toward a single feature while others alternate their gaze between single and multiple features. There are, in other words, individual differences in the manner in which even infants deploy attention.

One might categorize this approach to the visual world as overexclusive attention. There would be little or no incidental learning at this early age; conversely, one should not look for selective attention in the form in which we will find it later on in life. Now, if a child were to continue to use the perceptual mode of overexclusive attention at an age where most other children have developed beyond this phase, such a child would be severely handicapped in any learning task that requires more thorough exploration of the available stimuli. It is not inconceivable that some children do not develop beyond the level of overexclusive attention. Such profound retardation can be found in other areas of development; why not here? Maybe an extreme form of this kind of developmental retardation or fixation is represented by children with early infantile autism. These children have been described as manifesting "overselective responding" on tasks involving complex, multifaceted stimuli, and their learning is grossly impaired in almost every area. It is intriguing to speculate that early infantile autism is an extreme and all-pervasive form of learning disability and that it is due to a failure in the development of attentional processes.

OVERINCLUSIVE ATTENTION

In the course of normal development, children leave the phase of overexclusive attention where their attention is largely a function of the characteristics of the stimulus—its color, its size, or the fact that it is moving—and become capable of shifting attention more freely and more voluntarily. Many different aspects of the stimulus world now become the object of their attention—many more, in fact, than the minimum needed for truly efficient detection of the distinctive features. Incidental learning now reaches its highest point. Somewhere between the age of six and ten the normal child seems to learn as much about the incidental features as about the central features of a situation. This being the case, the amount of time they spend examining the central features is relatively less and from the point of view of efficiency, such overinclusive attention results in less than optimal information processing. It has been said of the typical ten-year-old that he "notices everything," sometimes to the amazement but often to the chagrin of elders.

Now a child who attends to many irrelevant stimuli will progress in focused learning, such as learning to read, more slowly than the child whose attention is less overinclusive. Since one should again find individual differences in the rate of development, some children at age eight, say, should still be closer to the level of overexclusive attention. They would get so engrossed with some single aspect of the printed page, such as the picture on it, that they would be unable to learn reading. Others, whose overinclusive attention developed early or was of particular intensity, would be attending to all the "wrong" things (from the teacher's point of view) and would be described as distractible. They, too, would have trouble doing what the school expects them to do, especially learning to read and other things that call for selective attention. In order to read with high efficiency one must attend to the relevant aspects of letter combinations and not to such irrelevant features as color or size of letters. Good readers in elementary school might be those children who are already in the next developmental phase, while poor readers might be those whose overinclusive attention is so dominant that they attend to too many irrelevant stimuli.

Indeed, some studies, in which children at various levels of reading proficiency have been compared on tasks measuring incidental learning, have found that good readers show less incidental learning than normal readers. If some children are poor readers because of their overinclusive attention, one of the methods that might be used to help them would be to limit the available stimuli to those which are relevant to the task, the letters on the printed page. Covering the pictures on the page, exposing only the line on which the child is to read, and screening the child from the distractions in the room have all been used with success with children who have this kind of problem.

SELECTIVE ATTENTION

Incidental learning undergoes a decline and selective attention thus seems to reach an optimal level after about age twelve. The youngster now seems able to select from the material in his or her environment those aspects which have been designated as central. Responses to irrelevant and incidental features are suppressed or inhibited, and information processing, such as reading, proceeds with ease—provided the student is one of those whose capacity to use selective attention has followed the expected developmental progress. Those children who reach that phase more slowly than others and still operate at the level of overinclusive attention would be seen as poor students. They would fail to meet performance expectations based on what the average child of that age should be able to accomplish. This discrepancy between expectation and performance would result in such children being described as learning disabled. If they also responded to stimuli which adults deem irrelevant, they might be called distractible and hyperactive. On the other hand, children who develop the capacity to sustain selective attention earlier than others, would be able, regardless of distraction, to concentrate their attention on a given task, and to shift their attention when this is called for by the task. It would stand to reason that this capacity is most valuable in the acquisition of academic subject matter and many good students may owe their success to this factor.

A DEVELOPMENTAL MODEL

In the development of a mature level of selective attention, the child passes through two earlier stages, the stage of overexclusive attention and the stage of overinclusive attention. With the individual differences in rate of development that one would have to expect, several different results could emerge. In Figure 2 we have tried to depict this speculative model. The child who remains fixated at the mode of overexclusive attention and still functions in this fashion at elementary-school age might be the autistic child. The child who enters this mode early might well be described as an alert baby. Those who move to overinclusive attention early and "notice everything" might be the children we call "interested"; those who remain in this mode long could be the distractible. The latter would probably turn out to be among the poor students, while those who had arrived early at the mode of selective attention would be at an advantage academically and thus be the good students. Lastly, there is the "normal child," the one who moves through the developmental phases neither too slowly nor too fast and by whose progress we tend to set our expectations for all others.

The developmental ideas reflected in Figure 2 are intended to underscore the conviction that differences in selective attention represent individual differences in the relative rates of development, and that they are not due to an absolute failure in development. Relatively slow development is not a defect or a deficit. It is a problem only because our expectations rarely take these individual differences into account. Some children simply reach a given level earlier, some later than others. Eventually all but a minute percentage should arrive at relatively similar levels—that is, provided they are given appropriate and, in some instances, highly specialized learning environments and that the pressures brought to bear on the more slowly developing child are not such that they create secondary problems, thus deflecting the child's development from its normal, though slower, course.

When a bright child lags behind peers and siblings in the

Figure 2
The Effect of Individual Differences in the Development of Selective Attention at Various Age Levels

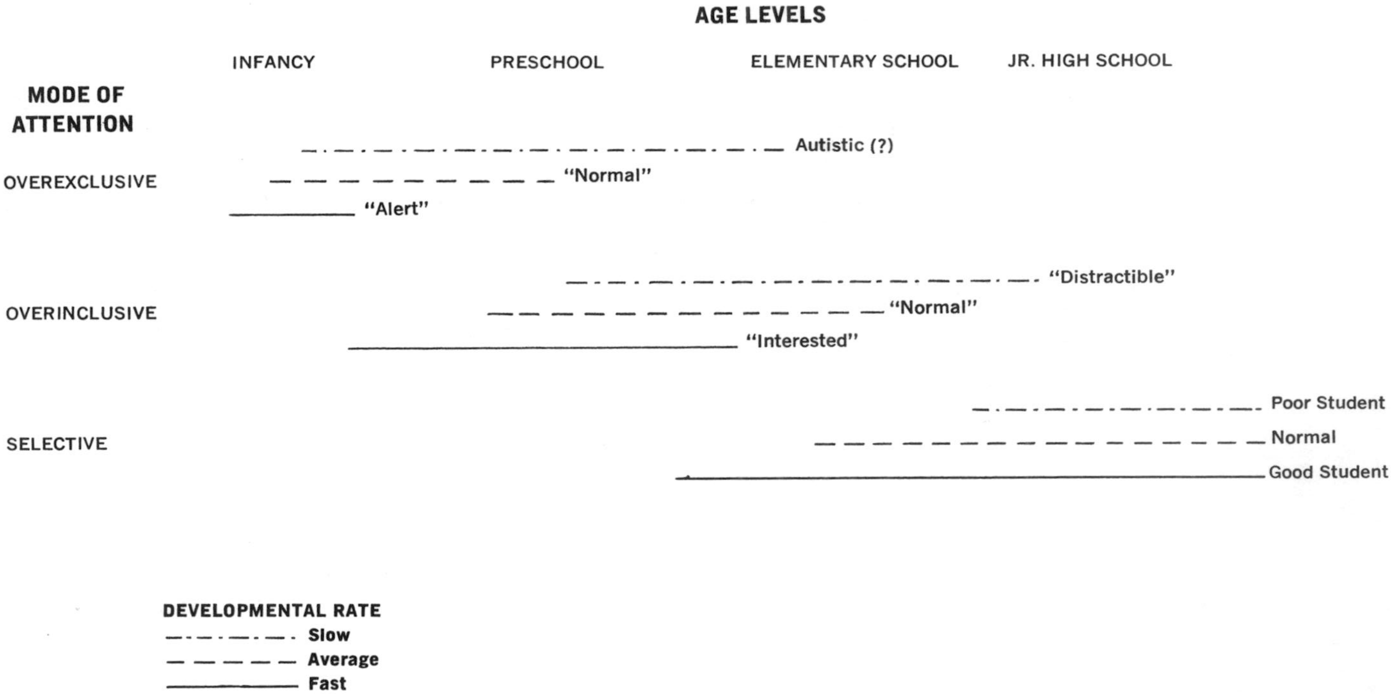

AGE LEVELS

INFANCY   PRESCHOOL   ELEMENTARY SCHOOL   JR. HIGH SCHOOL

MODE OF ATTENTION

OVEREXCLUSIVE

"Alert"   "Normal"   Autistic (?)

OVERINCLUSIVE

"Interested"   "Normal"   "Distractible"

SELECTIVE

Poor Student
Normal
Good Student

DEVELOPMENTAL RATE
·—··—·· Slow
— — — Average
——— Fast

acquisition of academic skills, parents and teachers almost always respond with consternation. They frequently assume that the failure is somehow the child's fault, that he or she is not paying attention, not working hard enough, or is lacking interest and motivation. They then put pressure on the child to do better, making the child feel inadequate, insecure, and anxious in any situation involving learning or taking tests. Such children then become more and more disorganized, and the older they get, unless they receive appropriate help, the more they will appear like the disorganized, anxious, inadequate-feeling child whose learning problems are caused by emotional problems. At that point, it becomes next to impossible to tease out cause and effect so that there is much confusion as to whether the emotional problem caused the learning problem or vice versa.

We would have to conclude, therefore, that every effort should be made to assess a child's developmental level with respect to selective attention as early as possible, and ideally before the child enters school, so that the mode and pace of teaching can be appropriate to the child's readiness to make use of it. Unfortunately, there is, at this point, no test or measure that is specifically designed to assess a child's maturity with respect to selective attention, and no school system explicitly includes that function in its assessment of reading readiness. We should be able to prevent most learning disabilities once we know how to match teaching to children's ability in the realm of selective attention. Until then, the best we can do is to work with learning-disabled children with ideas about selective attention clearly in mind.

Implications for Working with the Learning-disabled Child. A developmental formulation of selective attention and of its relation to learning disabilities has two corollaries. One is that we should expect that some learning-disabled children will "grow out of" their problems as they get older. Indeed, there are many reports from follow-up studies and clinical observations that the characteristic distractibility and hyperactivity of learning-disabled children decrease and disappear in early adolescence. The learning problems usually remain, however, but that is not surprising considering the cumulative nature of academic learning. If you have missed learning the expected material in elementary school, you are not likely to catch up all of a sudden when you get to junior high school. To say nothing of all the pressures such a child will have experienced in the first six or seven years of school which are likely to have resulted in anxiety about and dislike for school and negative attitudes about oneself and one's abilities. This leads to the second corollary of the developmental formulation.

If a child lags behind the peer group in the development of selective attention, we should not only adapt the way we teach to the child's rate of development, but we should also seek to help this development along by judicious structuring of the learning situation. Such structuring would have the goal of enhancing selective attention. To do this, three methods would seem to have merit. They involve increased distinctiveness of stimuli, rewards for selectively attending, and the teaching of response strategies.

INCREASED DISTINCTIVENESS OF STIMULI

Many beginning and poor readers have trouble distinguishing between similar stimuli. They confuse left and right, and up and down and thus can't tell *b* from *d*, *saw* from *was*, or *W* from *M*. If the teacher exaggerates the differences between such stimuli or introduces additional, relevant stimuli, such children can be helped. One can introduce highly similar stimuli in a series of graded steps where the critical features are first presented in isolation and irrelevant aspects are added gradually.

For example, three-year-old children are usually unable to differentiate between roundness and angularity; they thus have difficulty differentiating between the capital letters *U* and *V*. To teach them the difference one would begin by showing stimuli where the corners of the angular features and analogous portions of the rounded figures are emphasized, while the rest of the outline is barely visible. In succeeding trials, the outlines are made more and more pronounced until the initial emphasis on the critical difference (angle or roundness) disappears and the figure appears in its actual form. With such an approach, one can teach even very young and very retarded children to make difficult discriminations, for it gives them the opportunity for learning to attend to the relevant aspects of the stimulus.

Another way of helping children focus attention on the critical features of a visually presented stimulus is to have them learn to make careful comparisons. Children under five years of age often have great difficulty discriminating between visual stimuli that differ only in direction of orientation. It does not matter whether these stimuli are arrows, horseshoes, parentheses, or the letters *p, q, b,* and *d.* As the child gets older, the ability to differentiate between up and down improves but the difference between left and right continues to be a source of confusion. Children will thus acquire the ability to discriminate *b* from *p,* based on the direction of the stem, while *b* and *d* as well as *p* and *q* continue to be confused. Eventually, around age six, the average child learns to attend to both the up-down and left-right dimensions. In the case of these letters, the position of the stem and the position of the circle relative to the stem are now attended to and the correct identification takes place. However, children who are slower in this development will continue with the letter reversal, and this phenomenon is often found among disabled readers.

If one now takes children who confuse these similar letters and gets them to trace them or to align a stencil over them, they often learn the discrimination quite readily. This improvement has often been attributed to some perceptual changes which result from such "visual-motor training." It can be demonstrated, however, that it is not the child's motor movement but the accompanying observation of the details of the visual stimulus which makes the crucial difference. When the teacher places the stencil over the letters and points to the match or mismatch while explaining the relationship between the two stimuli, children learn as quickly as when they engage in the motor movement. Visual-motor exercises thus seem to work (when they work) because they enhance attention, not because they improve coordination.

Another way of enhancing attention is to present the relevant dimension of a stimulus in a variety of examples and in several forms. This is because the repeated presentation of the same form tends to reduce the effectiveness of a stimulus. We all know that if one hears or sees the same thing over and over again, one eventually adapts to it in such a way as to cease paying attention to it. If one wishes to teach a child the difference between *b* and *d,* one should not show the same pair of letters again and again. Instead, it would be wise to present this letter pair in a variety of sizes and in different degrees of brightness or color, as well as in different parts of the writing surface or written on such different surfaces as chalkboard, paper, and poster board.

The principle behind this approach is that children are more likely to attend to new rather than familiar stimuli, that novelty is a feature that increases attention, as do surprise, change, and a moderate amount of complexity. Competent teachers of young children have long known that their pupils can be kept attentive for a longer time if a task is presented in a novel, surprising, and changing way. Those charged with teaching learning-disabled children who have difficulties in sustaining selective attention would do well to adopt a similar approach.

REWARDS FOR SELECTIVELY ATTENDING

Since there is a limit to the amount of novelty even the most inventive teacher can bring to a simple task and since there are many routine and repetitious situations in which learning is nonetheless required, the addition of a reward can serve to maintain children's attention. The principle to be used here is to reinforce correct responses by quickly following them with the presentation of a reward that is meaningful to the child. Studies which used dichotic listening as a means of gauging selective attention of young children have shown that their performance can be improved (their selective attention enhanced) when the correct responses are reinforced. What is more, children will stay with even a dull task for a longer time if this results in some form of "payoff." For older children, this payoff may need to be no more than the immediate knowledge of whether their response was correct; for younger children more concrete rewards may be needed. In many instances, the function of a reward seems to be to provide the learner with feedback as to response accuracy. The motivational aspect of a reward may well be quite secondary. It is for this reason that rewards should be presented only when the correct response has been given, not for merely working on a task, regardless of the accuracy of the product. Giving "E" for "effort" is not a good policy when the goal is that the child learn to make the right responses.

TEACHING RESPONSE STRATEGIES

In addition to helping a child by modifying the way in which stimuli are presented and by reinforcing correct responses, one should also aim to teach the strategies necessary for producing the correct response. Selectively attending to the relevant stimulus dimensions is one such response strategy and, as we have repeatedly said, learning-disabled children appear not to have developed this strategy to a sufficient degree. It does not help such a child to be told, "Pay attention," or to be punished for not paying attention. What we must do is to teach what the child is to attend to and how one does that. Training in self-guidance has been shown to be an effective means of doing this. The child is taught to say, at first out loud, and later silently, statements such as, "To solve this kind of problem, I must stop and look and compare before I give an answer." Depending on the task, such a statement will include what is to be looked at and what is to be compared with what. Once more using the example of the *b-d* discrimination, the child might be taught to remind himself to look at the direction of the "bulge" and to compare it with the position of the upright line.

A related training procedure that focuses more directly on selective attention would teach the child, in essence, "don't look there, look here," where the *there* and the *here* have first been made distinctly different. "Don't look at the picture, look at the story" might be an example of this approach. This is far more effective than yelling at the child, "Pay attention to the story!"

TARGETING TRAINING PROCEDURES

The various approaches to teaching we have just sketched should not be applied indiscriminately to every child who needs special help. It has been one of the banes of education in general and special education in particular that a method which appears to work with one group of children comes to be used as a panacea for all children. It can be demonstrated, for example, that young children can be helped to learn a discrimination between similar stimuli if they are given words with which to label these stimuli. On the other hand, older children who have already acquired a fairly efficient use of selective attention seem to become distracted when they are made to label the stimuli.

Such developmental differences between children of different ages raise several related points that are well to keep in mind when planning a teaching approach. A technique that is of value when used with a young child who is learning a certain skill at a given age will not necessarily be helpful to an older child who failed to learn that skill at the appropriate age and is now in need of remedial or compensatory training. In fact, a technique that is helpful at the appropriate stage of development may be a hindrance when applied as a remedial method at a later stage. One always has to develop teaching methods that are appropriate for the age and condition of the prospective student. What works in teaching reading to a child in first grade will probably not work if used, without modification, in teaching reading to a ten-year-old with a reading disability. Nor is it likely to be of help to a semiliterate adult who tries to learn reading.

The reverse of what has just been said is also true. A strategy that is effectively used by a skilled adult in solving a given problem is not necessarily the ideal strategy to be used by a child who is in the process of acquiring that skill. Nor will such a strategy be necessarily helpful to someone who failed to learn the skill as a child and has to acquire it at a later age. Reading skill provides an obvious example for illustrating this point. The proficient adult reader decodes whole words or even word groups without attending to the individual letters in these words unless the word is highly unfamiliar. Thus "whole-word" reading is obviously very efficient and it should be the ultimate goal for any program designed to teach reading. It is unwarranted to assume, however, that the beginning reader had best not attend to the individual letters but learn to recognize the whole word instead. *The strategy used in the process of acquiring a skill is not the same as the strategy used once proficiency in that skill has been attained.* The same is probably true for problem readers who may have to unlearn inefficient or faulty strategies before they can proceed to work toward the acquisition of mature reading skills. For them, neither the approach used with the beginning reader in first grade nor that used by the proficient adult reader may be appropriate. Remedial methods must be designed for the specific purpose for which they are needed.

Thus, a teaching method that works with a young child will not necessarily work with an older child, and an approach used by a skilled adult is not necessarily the approach to use when teaching a child, whether or not that child has a learning problem. One further point bears mentioning in this connection. Some teaching methods are thought to work well with children who have learning problems, but their efficacy in that area should not lead one to believe that these methods are therefore appropriate for the teaching of children who do not have such a problem. It is by now well known that the selective and consistent use of rewards can serve to teach children behaviors they would otherwise have difficulty learning. But it would be a misguided parent who observes a child spontaneously doing something, like putting away his toys, and who now intrudes on the scene by giving the child a material reward for what he has done. Praise alone would be quite sufficient since the child is obviously already getting some inner satisfaction from engaging in the activity, a satisfaction which the reward may well serve to undercut. In short, what is appropriate for someone in need of help may be quite inappropriate for someone not in need of help, and vice versa.

Chapter 7

WHAT CAN BE DONE FOR THE LEARNING-DISABLED CHILD?

From the standpoint of the learning-disabled child, the most important question is not, "How did he get that way?" but, "What can we do for him?" Yet most parents and many teachers will, at one time or another, ask questions about the cause of the problem. For the time being, the best available answer to this question seems to be that learning-disabilities represent a developmental lag in the area of selective attention. Having explored this in the previous chapter, it is time that we turn to the more crucial issue: What can be done to help the learning-disabled child?

Parents of a learning-disabled child soon discover a rather dismal state of affairs. The number of opinions about their child is legion, yet most will focus on why the child is having difficulties, while few will have an answer to what should be done. The few who give an answer recommend medications, physical excercises, or perceptual-motor training, which, when tried, rarely lead to improvement in the area of greatest concern: the child's progress in school. The problem seems to be that when a child has difficulty in learning, whatever help we give must be aimed at relieving that difficulty; when a problem is in the classroom, the help we give must take place in the classroom. Indirect methods applied outside the classroom have not proven effective.

HOW DOES IT FEEL TO BE LEARNING DISABLED?

We can never really know how someone else feels. We can try to imagine it and we can assume that the other person feels the way we have felt in similar situations. When someone else has a problem which we don't have and never had, trying to imagine how that person feels is next to impossible. Our language is not very adequate for the communication of feelings. Children, in particular, are limited in their ability to describe how they feel. And yet, in order to understand and help a learning-disabled child, we should have some idea of how it feels to be learning disabled. Try the following exercise.

Take a pencil and a small tablet, about three by five inches, and stand in front of a mirror. Now hold the paper against your forehead and write your name on it with the pencil. Sounds easy?

The first thing you'll notice is that you can't hold the pencil in the usual fashion because if you do, you have trouble controlling its movement and difficulty seeing what you are writing. After finding a new way of holding the pencil you'll write your name without too much difficulty. Now look at the paper and see what you have written. You did not do what you had set out to do! The task was not to write the mirror image of your name. It was to write your name. Take a fresh piece of paper and try again.

Now imagine that there is someone standing over you who says, "Come on, that's not hard. Why don't you pay attention? What's the matter with you? You are not really trying. Everybody else is already finished!" This is what many learning-disabled children experience. How does it feel?

Now we will give you some special help. Help that takes your "problem" into account and teaches you the skill in a relevant manner.

Let's start with something easy. Don't write your name, write the word "good." And don't use script, but print it in capital letters. First you write it so it looks right in the mirror. Now, on the same sheet of paper, print the word again while looking at the one you have just finished, keeping in mind that you want it to come out looking correct when viewed directly and not in the mirror. When you check on what you have done, you may find that the G or D is still backward, but on the next try you'll be able to correct this error and now you will get it right every time you try. Doesn't that feel good? Now you may even want to go back to writing your name. You are lucky if it is Alan; if it is Catherine it will take a little longer.

Two Approaches

Turning to available research to find effective methods of helping children with learning disabilities, one finds them to come from the two dominant psychological approaches to the study of learning, the cognitive approach and the behavioral approach.

Learning, as we said in an earlier chapter, is an unobservable process that presumably has taken place inside the head when, following some experience, we are able to do something that we had been unable to do before. They psychologist who seeks to study learning by drawing inferences about this process and its operations is using a cognitive approach. Speculations about selective attention fall in this category.

Psychologists who favor a behavioral approach as the strategy to guide their research prefer to avoid inferences about internal processes. They look instead at the situation in which the learner is placed, the material that is presented, the answers that are given, and the consequences these answers have for the learner. The technical terms used for all this are by now quite familiar to most people. They are *stimulus, response,* and *reinforcement.*

While cognitive and behavioral psychologists are often placed in an adversary position, the two approaches are not so much competing as complementary. Whether one is a behavioral or a cognitive psychologist is not a matter of being right or being wrong, but a matter of a choice of strategy for the study of the phenomenon we call learning. Not too surprisingly, both approaches have therefore led to usable methods that can be applied in helping learning-disabled children learn.

Focus Determines Action. As we have said earlier, learning-disabled children have a number of characteristics which often accompany their problem in learning. Difficulty in sitting still is one of these characteristics, and this has resulted in the use of the descriptive terms *hyperactivity* or *hyperkinesis.* For some investigators, these terms have become the central focus of the problem, overshadowing the learning disability which, from the point of view of the child's future, is the far more critical issue. Another frequently observed characteristic of learning-disabled children is their tendency to blurt out the first thing that comes to mind instead of giving a question or problem careful consideration. The responses thus given are frequently wrong and the tendency has led people to speak of learning-disabled children as impulsive.

It is likely that both the trouble with sitting still and the tendency not to reflect before coming up with an answer to a question are consequences or correlates and not causes of the learning problems of these children. If a child attends to irrelevant stimuli and responds to them, that child may be observed to be hyperactive. If a child has discovered in the past that the answers given to teachers' questions are almost always wrong, and as a result becomes anxious when being asked a question, such a child can terminate that state more quickly by giving any old answer than by sitting, contemplating (while anxious), and arriving at the wrong answer at the end nonetheless.

The direction from which helping intervention is approached depends on how the problem of the learning-disabled child is construed. If the child's central problem is viewed as inadequate selective attention, strengthening that ability becomes the focus of remedial work. If the central problem is seen as hyperactivity, reducing the child's motor activity takes precedence over other remedial efforts, while those who view the central problem as impulsivity will seek to teach the child to be more reflective. Now only that, but on the formulation of the problem depends which children are selected for a study of the effectiveness of an intervention. Those investigators who emphasize hyperactivity select hyperactive children; those who emphasize selective attention pick children with attentional problems; those who emphasize learning disabilities select underachieving children; while those who emphasize impulsivity will look for that characteristic when they collect children for a study. The research literature in this field reveals that investigators have combined these characteristics in various ways so that it is rare for two different studies to address the same problem with the same kind of children. It is this diversity, among other difficulties, that makes for the confusion in this field and prevents anyone from arriving at conclusive answers to the questions that most trouble parents and teachers.

Behavioral methods of intervention focus on observable characteristics of children. As a result, investigators with this orientation often seek to modify what they can easily observe, such as the child's motor responses. Studies on hyperactivity are therefore often contributed by investigators with that orientation. The less easily observed characteristics of impulsivity and selective attention, on the other hand, are more likely to be studied by people who approach psychological problems with a cognitive orientation. Let us look at some representative studies under each of these rubrics and see what they might tell us about methods of helping learning-disabled children.

Cognitive Methods of Intervention

A group of investigators at Indiana University Medical School decided to explore whether children could be helped to be less impulsive if they were taught to "stop, look, and listen" before answering a question or responding to a task. Such training in self-command is thought to facilitate establishing for the impulsive child the kind of internal controls other children are able to use spontaneously.

Stop, Look, Listen, and Think! The children in the Indiana study were selected on the basis of their hyperactivity. On a test which involves the tracing of a paper-and-pencil maze they performed in a highly impulsive manner, making many careless errors in a rather haphazard way. The aim of the stop-look-listen training was to improve this maze test performance. As is so frequently the case in studies of this nature, the research focus is on an easily scored, readily administered, short-term task, not on the more important "real life" problems of the children: their learning problems in school. The latter, though much more critical than the ability to trace a maze, are far too complex to study in the confines of a single investigation, so that one must have patience with investigators who seek to chip away on the larger problems, one little piece at a time.

At any rate, the Indiana study showed that giving impulsive children training in self-command did succeed in improving their maze test performance. What was the nature of the training?

As a reminder of what the child was to say before beginning to work on a task, a card with instructions was placed on the table. This card read, "Before I start any of the tasks I am going to do, I am going to say: Stop! Listen, Look, and Think! *Before!* I answer." Cartoonlike illustrations emphasized these instructions and the child was asked to read the instructions aloud. The tasks used for training were different from the maze test which served as the criterion. One required the identification of identical figures, another involved finding hidden figures, and a third required the child to join with pencil lines a series of numbered dots.

The examiner-trainer who worked with the child would continually remind the child to read and follow the stop-look-listen instructions, both before a new task was introduced and when a page in the test booklet had to be turned. Before giving an answer the child would be expected to say, "I look and think before I answer." When the child failed to do this, the trainer would point to the reminder card, and insist that the child state the command before proceeding. When the child used the command spontaneously, he was praised with, "Good, you remembered the commands." After only two 30-minute sessions, given on two succeeding days, the children were retested with the mazes, and a comparison with a control group who had not received this training revealed a marked improvement in performance.

Other studies by the same and different investigators have repeatedly shown that children can be helped to acquire what might be termed self-control, if one teaches them to give themselves relevant verbal instructions. In the early phases of teaching these self-instructions, they must be said out loud because that is the only way to monitor whether the child does or does not make the statements. Later on, one can permit the child to say these words silently (to think them) because by then the child will have discovered that successful and rewarded performance depends on this strategy.

Teaching self-instruction can be done in the manner described above. It can also be accomplished by exposing the child to a model (either an adult or a child) who makes relevant verbal self-statements in connection with working on a task at which the model succeeds. Self-statements should probably go beyond the simple "stop, look, listen" used in the study described above. It is not enough for a so-called impulsive child to slow down before responding. The child must also learn what to do during the interval between the presentation of the task and initiation of the response. The Indiana study instructed the child to think. More to the point would be to teach the child what to think about. This was done in a well-known piece of research conducted by two investigators, D. Meichenbaum and J. Goodman.

Here the model would work on a task and say aloud such words as the following:

> Okay, what is it that I have to do? I am supposed to copy this picture. I have to go slow and be very careful. Okay. I draw the line down. Good. Then to the right. That's it. Now down some more and now to the left. Good. I'm doing fine so far. Now I have to go back up again. Oops, no, I was supposed to go down. That's okay. I just erase the line carefully. . . . Good. Even if I make an error I can still go slowly and carefully. Okay, I have to go down now. That's it. I'm finished. I did it.

As the child observes a model behaving in this manner, the details of a strategy can be acquired. When the child is then asked to do what the model has just done, these self-verbalizations become a part of his or her way of approaching tasks of this nature. Improved performance thus made possible held up over a period of four weeks, but the improvement was limited to paper-and-pencil tasks that were similar to those on which the training had taken place. As far as the children's classroom behavior was concerned, they were as poor in self-control, activity level, and cooperation after the two-week program as before. That, of course, should not be too surprising. Why should one expect that training a child to be more careful on a paper-and-pencil task will somehow result in more appropriate classroom behavior? Just as we have said earlier that it makes no sense to expect that teaching a child to walk blindfolded on a balance beam (as is done in some perceptual-motor training programs) will improve that child's reading, so one should not expect that training in the copying of line drawings will lead to sitting still in class. If one wants a child to read better, one has to teach reading; if one wants a child to sit still more often, one has to teach sitting still. There are no shortcuts and there is no magic.

"Here's How." It is of little help to an impulsive child to be told "take your time," "stop and think," or "be careful." All these admonitions do no more than to convey the instruction not to be impulsive; they state, in effect, what the child should *not* be doing. If one really wishes to help such a child, one has to teach him or her the positive steps which will lead to success in the task at hand. This was clearly demonstrated in a study where one group of impulsive children was instructed to wait 10 to 15 seconds before responding and to "think about your answer and take your time." Another group of these children was taught a set of specific rules and basic strategies which they were to follow in producing their responses to the tasks on which they were being trained. These tasks involved matching geometric designs, comparing nonsense words, drawing designs from memory, and describing geometric designs in words. The rules and strategies the second group of children were being taught were designed to help them focus on the relevant features of the stimuli, to examine alternatives, to examine component parts of the problem, to look for similarities and differences, and to eliminate alternative answers until only the correct one remained. In short, the training was designed to enhance selective attention. Compared to the group that merely had been told to delay their response, the second group learned what they should do during the delay. The focus was not on impulsivity but on response strategy.

Two months after the children in both groups had been given eight 30-minute training sessions spread over a period of four weeks, they were reexamined with a test called the Matching Familiar Figures test. This instrument permits the classification of children in terms of their impulsive or reflective response style. On this test, all these children had originally been shown to be impulsive in that they quickly produced a lot of wrong answers. The reexamination revealed that the children who had been trained merely to delay their responses before answering were again as impulsive as they had been before they received training; the children who had been taught what to do during the delay, the ones who had been taught a response strategy, had become much more reflective. They were able to give more correct answers and to do so less impulsively.

In view of the fact that no other study had up to then demonstrated salutary effects of laboratory interventions on classroom performance, it is of particular interest that, compared to the "take-your-time" group, the children who had been taught a response strategy achieved significantly higher scores on a test of reading comprehension five months after the training had been completed.

What Is Impulsiveness? The results of this study suggest that the problem of these children was not impulsiveness but an underdeveloped ability to use selective attention. Once they had been taught to attend selectively to the relevant aspects of the stimuli and to focus on components for clues, they were able to give correct answers and, incidentally, were no longer impulsive. That is, they no longer blurted out the wrong answer. It does seem, as we suggested in the last chapter, that this blurting out of the wrong answer is a way these children have learned for getting out of the anxiety-arousing situation produced by being faced with the task they know, from experience, to be insolvable. This speculation is supported by the fact that in the study just summarized even the improved children would revert to the so-called impulsive mode of responding when they encountered more difficult problems. Thus, under conditions where they anticipated failure, the old way of behaving reemerged, just as one would predict if one assumed that impulsivity is a response style which had been learned under those conditions.

Behavioral Methods of Intervention

The behavioral orientation calls for a focus on directly observable behavior. For this reason, many studies conducted by psychologists with this orientation have had their focus on the motor behavior (hyperactivity) of learning-disabled children. One can readily observe (and count) getting up from the seat, turning around, looking up, tapping on the desk, or making noise—far more readily, at any rate, than whether a student is selectively attending to the relevant aspect of the material the teacher is presenting. As we shall see, however, even attention—now called attending behavior—can be defined in such a way as to make it observable.

Behavior Is a Function of Its Consequences. Why the stress on the observable? The behavioral psychologist operates on the assumption that behavior is a function of its consequences, that the events that immediately follow a given act will determine whether this act will or will not be repeated when similar circumstances again present themselves. If, from the point of view of the person who performs the act, the consequence was positive, the act is likely to be repeated. On the other hand, if the consequence was negative, or if it had no consequence at all, the act is less likely to be performed again. In other words, rewards tend to strengthen behavior; punishment or the absence of consequences tends to weaken it.

Given these assumptions, anyone seeking to influence a person's future behavior would have to arrange matters in such a way that desirable acts are followed by positive consequences, while changeworthy behavior is followed by negative consequences or nothing at all. Furthermore, the more immediately the consequence is brought to bear, the more powerful will be its effect. This is where the need for observation enters the picture. Unobserved events cannot be immediately reinforced, so that if one seeks to influence behavior, one must be able to know exactly when it is taking place.

Whether a given consequence is positive, and thus rewarding, or negative, and thus punishing, depends on the individual to whom the consequence is happening. We should be guided by the ancient wisdom of Lucretius that what is food to one may be fierce poison to others. Never assume that something is reinforcing until its effectiveness as a reinforcer has been demonstrated with the child whose behavior is to be influenced. A hug, a kiss, a penny, or a piece of candy may be positive consequences to many children, but there are children for whom any or all of these are either meaningless or even unpleasant experiences. Some children, in fact, seem to find it reinforcing to be scolded or reprimanded. More of that later. Suffice it to say here that many attempts to use reinforcement for changing behavior have failed because the presumed reinforcements being used were, in fact, meaningless or negative consequences.

"Put Not Your Trust in Vinegar—." Behavioral psychologists believe that it is more effective in the long run to strengthen desirable behaviors by positive reinforcement than to attempt to weaken undesirable behaviors by punishment or the withdrawal of previously available positive consequences. This belief is based not only on a humanistic aversion to the use of punishment but also on experiments which have shown that punishment maintains its effect only as long as the punishing agent or the situation in which the punishment was meted out remain present. What is more, the use of punishment has many negative side effects, not the least of which is that the person who has been punished will tend to fear the person who has done the punishing. Since it is difficult to teach if the intended student is afraid of, hates, or avoids the teacher, behavioral psychologists advocate the use of rewards wherever feasible.

"—Molasses Catches Flies!" Fortunately, from the point of view of helping children with behavioral methods, all undesirable behavior that one might wish to reduce has its desirable opposite that one would wish to increase. Thus, a boy who is constantly out of his seat can be worked with not by punishing the out-of-seat behavior but by rewarding whatever brief moments he may be spending sitting down. "Catch them when they are good" is excellent advice for parents and teachers. Unfortunately, most of us tend to react to undesirable behavior and to ignore the desirable, taking it for granted. This is partic-

ularly true of the irritating, disruptive behavior of hyperactive children. We attend to them (and thus probably reinforce them) when they move about, but we hardly ever take note of the few moments when they are sitting quietly. If we could but reverse this tendency, ignoring the wiggling and rewarding the quiet moments, we could probably achieve our objectives much more readily. That was clearly demonstrated, at any rate, in the case of Raymond.

Raymond. Raymond was ten years old. He was hyperactive, had a short attention span, disrupted class, and often fought with other children. He would spend most of his time in the classroom staring into space, walking about the room, almost continuously moving his arms or legs, and generally failing to attend to the academic tasks. All of these behaviors are observable, of course, and counting them revealed that, on the average, Raymond made approximately five of these "nonattending responses" per minute.

Both the recording of his behavior and the subsequent steps used to change it required that an observer be placed in the classroom. Having told Raymond that they wished to teach him to sit still so that he could study better, the psychologists gave him some earphones to wear through which, via a small radio receiver worn on his belt, they could signal to him that he had earned a reward. The rewards (small pieces of candy) were to be earned for every ten-second period during which the boy did not display any nonattending responses. Raymond's classmates were told that the boy was wearing the equipment so that he could learn to sit still. They were also told that he would be earning candy and that he would share this with the class at the end of the period (because the "rate of exchange" was such that he would earn far more than he could possibly consume by himself). In this manner, the support of the boy's classmates was solicited and they did indeed contribute their praise and cheers for his successes.

After three weeks during which this procedure was followed, Raymond was observed to make significantly fewer disruptive responses. Instead of the five per second he had made at the beginning, his rate was down to 3.3 per second, which, considering the brief period of treatment, represents a marked improvement. Had the program been continued, this child's hyperactivity might well have been reduced even further.

Working with one child at a time, using a special observer with radio transmitter, radio receiver, and earphones, is clearly not a method which lends itself for use in the regular classroom. Thus, it is good to know that behavioral methods have been used with success when applied to groups of disruptive children and without fancy hardware. When this is done, teachers, or aides, or even the students themselves hand out tokens, such as plastic disks, checkmarks, or paper scrip for instances of clearly specified, desirable behavior. When these reinforcers are handed out, their delivery is always accompanied by statements of praise, approval, smiles, and other social gestures which can then continue to be used as reinforcers when the more artificial tokens are later eliminated. While the tokens are in use, it is understood that the children can exchange them after class or at the end of the day for various so-called back-up reinforcers. These are items children value, such as small toys, food, or various special privileges.

Such a procedure, though it requires careful planning by people who understand the principles of behavior, is easy to communicate both to children and nontechnically trained adults. There have been demonstrations which used other children, adult volunteers, or parents as training agents. It can also be shown that improvement in behavior lasts beyond the initial training sessions and carries over into the regular classroom, provided some (or all) of the training took place in that setting. Since it is relatively easy to institute, there is no reason why the regular classroom should not be the setting for teaching children the behavior thought appropriate for that classroom. Problems should be treated where they occur. The tendency to remove a problem child from the classroom in order to "get treated" in somebody's clinic or consulting room is probably responsible for the relatively poor track record of such referrals.

Behavior Abhors a Vacuum. One of the risks in blindly reinforcing instances of nondisruptive behavior is that the child will merely learn to sit still and thus to look as if he or she were paying attention. Whenever one works on reducing the frequency of something undesirable, one must simultaneously work toward establishing the desirable alternative that is to take its place.

Visualize a pie diagram that represents the total time in a child's school day. A "slice" representing one quarter of this time might be taken up with disruptive, undesirable behaviors. In a program aimed at reducing this behavior, say by no longer paying any attention to it and thus withdrawing reinforcement from the disruption, this undesirable behavior might well vacate its time slice, but something—some other behavior—will have to fill that space. There cannot be a behavioral vacuum. For this reason it is important that a person who plans such a program of behavior change decide not only on how to reduce undesirable behavior but also on what desirable behavior is to be put in its place. Unless one makes explicit and systematic plans to develop behavior to fill the "space" vacated by the undesirable, the behavior most likely to move into the vacant time slot is whatever happens to be reinforced, often by chance, at that particular moment. This is as likely to be some new undesirable behavior as something constructive.

When one works with a hyperactive child on reducing the hyperactivity by means of a behavioral program, one can reward and thus increase the periods of sitting still. But merely sitting still should not be the goal of the program. Sitting still is merely a necessary step toward attending to the material being taught. For this reason, the child should be rewarded not merely for sitting still, but for sitting still *and* working on the task at hand. Otherwise, one is apt to end up with a child who has simply learned to "sit still and do nothing."

How the Parent Can Help

One of the most attractive aspects of behavioral methods of intervention is the straightforward logic of the principles involved. Folk wisdom has long held that one can catch more flies with honey than with vinegar, and it is true that one can accomplish far more with positive reinforcement than with punishment. Once the validity of this statement has been accepted, one need only identify the "flies" one wishes to catch. They are, of course, the desirable behavior we all too often take for granted and think about only when it is absent.

Parents can readily learn the basic principles of reinforcement and thus carry out or participate in the treatment of their own child. It is not always possible, for example, for a teacher to hand out in the classroom the rewards a child has earned in any given period. For this reason, a teacher using behavioral methods may give the child only checkmarks on a piece of paper, each mark representing an occasion when the child has earned reinforcement for desirable behavior. These checkmarks can then be traded for more concrete rewards once the child gets home. This has the advantage that the rewards can be highly personalized and consistent with the family's values, standards, and economic position. More importantly, however, parents can and should add their own praise and expressions of pleasure for the number of "points" the child has earned. This so-called social reinforcement should of course continue to be used as reward long after the child has finished participation in the special behavioral program. In that sense, the parents provide a bridge between the special program (or special class) and the usual situation in the regular classroom.

An exciting example of the effectiveness of a program of this nature appeared in the publication *Exceptional Children* in 1968. There were ten students who attended a special class for children with learning disabilities. They all were working at least two years below their age-appropriate grade level in one or more academic subject matters. They were all described as highly distractible and prone to engage in disruptive behavior. Instead of focusing on this undesirable behavior, however, the psychologists chose completion of work assignments as the target of their intervention. Accordingly, the children were given weekly grades and their parents were instructed to award a monetary allowance, the size based on the level of the grade. For example, each A would earn ten cents, each B five cents, each C one cent and an Incomplete would result in the loss of ten cents. The actual amounts used in this pay scale were set by the parents on the basis of the family economy and values. The weekly exchange of grades for money was to be a special and important event. The child was henceforth expected to pay for all highly valued, personal items with the money thus earned.

At the end of the school year all ten of the students who had participated in this program were working successfully one to four grade levels higher than where they had started in all academic areas. Six of them had returned to full-time attendance in regular class, one grade higher than where they had been during the previous year. All of these children now consistently earned at least C averages, with half of them obtaining B averages. At the end of the following year, all six of these once learning-disabled children were promoted to the next grade.

Most children seem to find it rewarding to receive an occasional comment that reflects the quality of the work they are doing. They are thus able to keep on working even though the ultimate "payoff" is no more than a grade on a report card, given at the end of a relatively long period of time. Some children can't wait that long for their reinforcers and it is they who need special attention. In the study just cited, feedback and reinforcement was provided on a weekly basis, but even that may not be sufficient for children whose long-standing learning problems have led them to get very little out of—which is another way of saying, get very little reinforcement from—working on academic tasks. For children with such low motivation one must therefore design a program where reinforcement is given even more frequently than once a week.

Tokens and Prizes. Why is it that the letter *A* or the number 100 written on a piece of paper, called a report card, is such a rewarding experience? Intrinsically, these symbols have no value. How did they acquire value? The answer lies in the fact that in the course of a child's experience these symbols have come to stand for something else. When a card player is happy when winning a pile of plastic disks, it is not the disks that cause the happiness but the fact that these can be traded for money. Poker chips have no value in and of themselves; they are tokens which stand for something else, something that has value. The pieces of paper or metal we call money have no intrinsic value either; they are tokens which derive their value from the fact that they can be exchanged for the things we "really" want. These things may be comfort, pleasure, the admiration of others, or—in the final analysis—the basic essentials of life: food, clothing, and shelter. The tokens we call money thus serve as rewards and as payment for the work we do, and our entire economy is based on these tokens. One might say that we have a token economy—the kind of economy psychologists have set up in situations where they wish to reward behavior of people for whom the rewards which motivate most of us (a sense of accomplishment, praise from others, a smile, or a "thank you") are, for some reason, not effective.

A good grade on a report card is a token, just like poker chips or a dollar bill are tokens. A good grade has acquired reinforcing properties for a child because bringing one home in the past has been the occasion for receiving smiles, hugs, and kisses from a parent whose smiles, hugs, and kisses have already had reinforcing properties, presumably because they, in turn, were in the past associated with other nice and pleasant things, maybe going back as far as receiving milk as an infant. Since the reinforcing properties of a token, such as an A on a report card, must have been acquired through a series of related experiences, it stands to reason that for some children this series has somehow gone awry so that an A is meaningless, particularly if it is never received or very rarely and then only after a considerable period of time has elapsed between doing the good work and receiving the grade. The effectiveness of a reinforcer is greatest when it is delivered immediately after the response it is meant to reinforce. In that sense the report card at the end of a marking period is a very weak reinforcer for many children. It is here that a token program can be most helpful and where the cooperation of teachers and parents becomes immensely important.

An interesting example of the use of token reinforcements which were delivered with minimal delay took place in a school in Michigan. There were seven children in a class who had a variety of problems, ranging from poor academic performance in reading, spelling, and arithmetic to inattentiveness and talking out of turn. The tokens in this case took the form of a daily report card system in that the child would be given a note at the end of the day which said, for example, "Your child did very well in arithmetic today." The parents had been asked to give the children some special reward when such notes were brought home. These rewards differed for different children;

some involved special privileges such as staying up to watch a favorite TV program, others entailed coveted snacks, small toys, or even money. These so-called backup reinforcers will vary from child to child, depending on what the child values, and they must of course be made available when, but only when, the required token is brought home. Otherwise the tokens lose their value; the economy breaks down.

In the Michigan study, six of the seven children showed significant improvement in their school performance. The effectiveness of this approach has been demonstrated in a variety of settings, using a variety of token-back-up reinforcer combinations. In instances where even a daily report card involves too great a delay between the performance of the work and the obtaining of the reward, teachers have dispensed plastic disks or checkmarks on a special card, giving these right at the child's desk and immediately upon completion of an assignment. These tokens were then traded at the end of the day for a note to the parents who, in turn, awarded the individualized reinforcer which was gauged to the child's interests and the family's value system and economic circumstances.

While the specifics of a token program will vary, the basic considerations are the same. First, the children must be told explicitly what kind of behavior will earn a token. The criteria for this should be as objective as possible. It is not enough to say that "good work" will earn a reinforcer; one must define what one considers "good." Number of problems correctly solved, number of lines written with fewer than a specified number of errors, number of minutes of staying quietly in one's seat are the kind of specific criteria needed in order to avoid the ambiguity which leads to argument and injustice. In the beginning these requirements may have to be quite minimal. They can be gradually extended as the children acquire proficiency. What is vital is that the reinforcers be dispensed with regularity, consistency, and in a systematic fashion.

Once the occasions for earning tokens have been specified and the means for dispensing them decided upon, the second consideration involves the rules under which the tokens are to be exchanged for back-up reinforcers. In some residential schools this exchange can take place in a special "store" where the children can go after class to "purchase" their desired prizes. In most schools, however, the parents must participate in the program if it is to work. They must recognize the importance of the fact that the availability of back-up reinforcers must be as regular, consistent, and systematic as the dispensing of the original tokens. The "bank" must not be closed when the child wants to exchange the currency, nor must the market be flooded with the back ups so that the currency loses its value. This often entails considerable inventiveness on the part of parents who must be willing to provide the child with privileges which had not previously been available, for it is better not to restrict the opportunities which up to then had been freely available in order to make them contingent on the payment of the new token currency.

"But Isn't That a Bribe?" When one describes a behavioral program based on reinforcement principles, the question most frequently asked and the objection most often heard has to do with the notion of a bribe. If children are told (as they are in these programs) that certain behaviors will earn them a reward, is that not a bribe? And is it really a good idea to use bribes to get children to behave in a correct or desirable manner?

Bribes are surely bad. They corrupt both the giver and the receiver, and in relation to officials or other people in authority, they are, in fact, illegal. What then is the difference between giving a police officer money for tearing up a summons and giving a child money for bringing home a good grade? Both are rewards for work that has been done and in that sense, both are reinforcements.

The difference between rewarding the police officer for ignoring a violation and rewarding a child for completing his homework lies in the ethical value of the behavior being reinforced. The police officer who accepts a bribe is being rewarded for something he should not be doing. A bribe is unethical and illegal because it reinforces unethical or illegal behavior. The child who receives a reward is being reinforced for something he should be doing, something desirable that is neither unethical nor illegal, be that homework, or cleaning up a room, or taking out the garbage. Reinforcement is right or wrong, good or bad only in terms of the behavior in question. If the behavior is wrong, reinforcement is wrong, and it is the wrong behavior that a bribe is reinforcing that gives the bribe its negative implication.

"Why Reward Doing One's Duty?" To say that we are reinforcing a child for something he or she *should* be doing raises a related question. If the child should be doing something like cleaning up his room, why introduce reinforcement? The word "should" seems to imply a moral imperative. The child should be doing the right thing for the sake of doing right; why offer a reward for doing one's duty? In order to answer that question, we must ask ourselves why *we* tend to do our duty, do the right thing since we don't ordinarily get rewarded for doing so. If asked, most of us would probably say that our motivation for doing the right thing is that it makes us feel good. We either experience pride, satisfaction, or righteousness for having done the "proper" thing, or we feel relief for having avoided the consequences we would probably suffer had we behaved improperly. These consequences might be feelings of guilt, social criticism, shame, punishment, embarrassment, or any of a number of negative experiences which tend to keep us on the straight and narrow. This, of course, means that somewhere, sometime we have learned that behaving in the proper fashion leads to positive consequences or to the avoidance of negative consequences. It is pretty certain that people are not born knowing right from wrong, proper from improper.

In the case of the child who is not doing what he or she should be doing, who is not doing the proper thing, one must assume that, for some reason, the relationship between such behavior and its consequences has not yet been learned. Since the intrinsic motivations that make us do the right and proper things are not available to that child, we must—for a time— introduce extrinsic motivations so that the child can learn what the rest of us already know: Doing the right thing leads to good consequences. We would not need to pay the child a quarter for taking out the garbage if taking out the garbage made him feel good inside because he views it as his contribution to the running of the household. That good feeling inside may develop eventually if the quarter is not paid perfunctorily but in relation to indications of pleasure and acceptance which communicate to the child that it is nice to be a member of a smoothly running household.

"How Long Will This Go On?" Two other issues are related to this discussion of establishing desirable behavior by means of positive reinforcement. One takes the form of the question, "But will I have to pay him henceforth and ever after for doing his homework?" and the other has to do with the effect on other children if one is singled out for such special treatment.

The question about how long a reinforcement policy has to be continued is to be found in how long it will take for the child to find the particular activity (homework) to have other reinforcing consequences. Once the child discovers that completing homework assignments leads to better grades and that better grades lead to other good things, the artificial reinforcement represented by the monetary reward can be discontinued. At that point, it probably should be absorbed in a more general allowance that is paid to a child for making specified, constructive contributions to a harmonious family life. Like a parent's salary, a child's allowance should be related to a definite job that has been well done. It should not come to be viewed as something due to the child as a matter of course.

"And What about Her Brother?" This point essentially serves as the answer to the question about the effect on other children. All members of a household have their jobs, duties, or responsibilities, and all should receive appropriate rewards for these. Obviously, these rewards need not be monetary in nature. They can take the form of affection, privileges, or opportunities, but the relationship between the job and the consequences should be understood by everyone and no one should have the impression that somebody else is being rewarded for something that is taken for granted when they do it. Nobody's work should ever be taken for granted.

Chapter 8

WHAT ABOUT THE CHILD WHO REFUSES TO GO TO SCHOOL?

School Refusal

There is no necessary connection between learning disabilities and school refusal, except that both have to do with the child's school experience and, on occasion, a child who is not doing well in his or her academic work may refuse to attend classes. Children who refuse to go to school, like any other children engaging in any other kind of behavior, are not a homogeneous group. The only thing any two of them could have in common may be that neither is in class when class attendance is expected. The term *school refusal* is thus a general and descriptive term, and we must investigate the specific circumstances before we can know what any particular child's school refusal is all about.

On closer inspection, one can discriminate three kinds of school refusal and each has a distinctive label: truancy, school phobia, and separation anxiety. Let us look at each of these in some detail, for we shall find that each has its own implications and that each calls for different remedial measures.

Truancy. Truancy is essentially an administrative, quasi-legal term and, as such, it is used by school authorities to label a child who repeatedly and continuously stays away from school without permission. Because the law demands school attendance, the truant (and the parent who condones the behavior) is subject to legal sanctions and intervention by the court. Because parents are expected and in fact may be ordered by the court to see to it that children attend school, truancy is frequently a struggle which pits the child against the combined forces of parents, school, and courts.

This often makes that kind of school refusal not so much a matter of explicit verbal dissent, as one of clandestine activities. The child may set out from home in the morning ostensibly on the way to school and return at the appropriate time as if coming home from school. Unsuspecting parents may thus be quite unaware of the fact that their child is not attending classes. Often they don't find out until someone from the school inquires about the child's whereabouts.

Whether and how soon such an inquiry takes place depends a great deal on the nature of the school. In a more affluent school district, where careful attendance records are kept on a daily basis, the principal's office or the school nurse may be on the phone to the child's home within two hours of the first day of unexplained absence. In such a school district it is very likely that the child's family has a telephone and that someone will be at home to answer it. In the crowded classroom in a less affluent school system, the harried teacher may not discover the absence of a particular child for several days. The person responsible for looking into this, be it a vice principal, a nurse, a social worker, or an attendance (truant) officer, is likely to have such a long list of problems with which to deal that the absent child may be one of their lesser worries. The chances are that the child's home has no telephone and even if there is one, the parent, being at work, may not be there to answer it. Days and weeks may go by before someone can go to the house and remedial action, therefore, is long delayed.

It should by now be clear that the kind of school refusal we call truancy and what is done about it has a great deal to do with the socioeconomic status of the child's family. This is true not only in terms of the time lag between the child's failure to attend class and how quickly something is done about it; it is also true in the very use of the label *truant* itself. A truant is a child who stays out of school *without permission*. If a child stays away from school *with* permission, he or she is not a truant, but something else. What? One possibility is "a case of school phobia"; that is, the child has been given a respectable sounding, quasi-medical diagnosis for the very same behavior that leads others to be called truants. Since a medical diagnosis justifies the absence from school, it makes the absence permissible, hence, not truancy. Thus, it may be that, in some instances, the difference between truancy and school phobia is no more than a difference in the economic background of the child's family. If the family can afford to have the child attend an affluent school where absences are immediately noticed and if they can then seek out a physician who "diagnoses" the problem, the case is called school phobia; if not, it becomes truancy. The truant is a "bad" child who must be punished; the school phobic is a "sick" child who must be cured. As so often, the label determines how we view people and what we do to or for them.

School Phobia. Since a phobia is an overwhelming and disabling fear of a specific situation or object, a school phobia, in its technical sense, is an overwhelming fear of school that makes it impossible for the child to attend classes. When such a fear is not present, when the child simply "doesn't feel like going," when potential failure is being avoided, or when other activities are more attractive than school, the use of the term school phobia is inappropriate. On occasion, unfortunately, the term is misused by parents, school authorities, or misguided physicians who wish to find an acceptable explanation for a child's refusal to go to school. The learning-disabled child who experiences one failure after another and thus finds school a very unpleasant place to be may wish, understandably, to avoid these experiences by no longer going to school. It obviously would be a disservice to such a child to be called school phobic when what is needed, and was for a long time, is specialized help with learning.

HOW DOES SCHOOL PHOBIA START?
Even when one has isolated genuine school phobia from other conditions which should not come under that heading, the children in this category are still of many kinds. One major

difference, of course, is in the child's age. Children in the early elementary school grades who express fear of going to school for the first time are different from older youngsters who often have been troubled about going to school for many years. We shall here concentrate on the young school-phobic child where the reason for the onset is often quite apparent and where remedial action is relatively simple.

It is not unusual for the young school-phobic child to complain about such physical problems as headaches, stom-achaches, or nausea. Such children also frequently express fears about a variety of other things, such as darkness. They are, in other words, generally fearful children whose fears have come to focus around school. The physical complaints are not difficult to understand. Strong fears can make one's head or stomach hurt. So the phobic child may not be faking physical discom-fort; the physical discomfort may be real, though not based on physical illness. In addition, however, most children learn quite early that the quickest way for eliciting mother's concern and sympathy is to complain of aches and pains. And when you have aches and pains you don't go to school.

AN OUNCE OF PREVENTION

It is very likely that school phobia is a mixture of real fears and a variety of learned ways of responding to stress. At one time or another, nearly every child will have expressed a reluctance to go to school. Whether this is worded, "Mommy, do I have to go to school today?" or "Today I'm going to stay home with you" or "I don't want to go to school today," most parents will have been faced with such a situation. Those who have dealt with it in a matter-of-fact way, insisting that school attendance is not only expected but also required—"Sometimes we all have to do things we don't feel like doing. Off you go!"—will probably have heard no more about it. In fact, the occasion will have been a constructive experience for the child since it taught that we can't always do what we feel like doing.

On the other hand, parents who entered into lengthy dis-cussions, making detailed inquiries into why the child does not want to go to school, will undoubtedly have elicited more or less plausible and more or less factual rationalizations. At that point, they were in a dilemma. What does one do when the child pleads a stomachache or a headache or makes a statement such as, "The teacher doesn't like me"? Now one either has to belittle this reason (and with it, the child) or one has to make further inquiries which may well lead to the parent's acceding to the child's wish to remain home. At that point, the basis for future school refusals may well have been laid. Having once learned that complaining about a stomachache results in the pleasant consequence of staying home, thereby avoiding the less pleasant experience of going to school, complaints about stomachaches become more likely.

Being home with mother, particularly if she takes extra good care of the child who could not go to school because of a stomachache, is a pleasant, hence reinforcing event. Compared to that, going to school is bound to be unpleasant. The balance is thus weighted in favor of staying home. With every day of staying home, this balance shifts further in that direction, for returning to school, after having been absent for a day or so, becomes more and more unpleasant because the child will now fear that, having fallen behind, the work will be more difficult. Thus, there is a snowball effect which will make it increasingly more difficult to get the child back to school until, finally, a full-blown "school phobia" is established.

The parents, faced with a child who complains about physical discomfort or mentions something unpleasant that happened at school in justification of wishing to stay at home, do, of course, have a difficult decision to make. What if the child is really sick or if the situation at school is truly intolerable? Once such complaints have been elicited they deserve being investigated. Some parents let the fever thermometer serve as the basis of the decision. "If you have no temperature, off to school you go." Others will seek an appointment with their pediatrician and if no medical reason is found, take the child directly from the physician's office to the school. Where complaints have to do with attacks by other children or teachers' hostility, the responsible parent will seek to ascertain what is real and what is an exaggeration on the part of the child. There is no denying that this is not always easy, but no one has ever claimed that being a parent is always easy.

Most psychological problems of childhood are found far more frequently among boys than among girls. School phobia is one of the few exceptions. Here the incidence among girls is at least as great, if not greater, than among boys. Why should this be? The answer, we suspect, lies in the different expectations we hold for boys and for girls. Who is more likely to be permitted to stay at home because of a complaint about attacks by other children or similar unpleasant experiences? Boy or girl? Who is more likely to be told to "stand up for your rights" or not to "act like a baby," boy or girl? Chances are that, despite recent presumed changes in our attitudes which have received a lot of publicity but little substantiation, mothers continue to be more compassionate with girls than with boys. It is, of course, also possible that there still lingers in many families the old attitude that school (with its preparation for earning a living) is more important for boys than for girls.

When school-phobic children are seen at clinics, a complaint that is frequently heard has to do with embarrassment in connection with undressing for gym classes. Again, this is more frequently a problem for girls than for boys, and one suspects that it too is related to our culture. Standards of modesty are different for boys and for girls, and we tend to be more accepting of a girl's than of a boy's hesitation in this area. All this might result in reinforcement for not going to school being more readily available for girls than for boys, thus the relatively higher incidence of school phobia among girls.

WHAT TO DO?

The most important principle in dealing with a child in the first three or four grades who expresses fear of school and has begun to refuse to go to school is to insist that school attendance be resumed. The longer a child remains away from school, the more difficult it will be to reverse the trend of school refusal and the more likely it is that a full-blown school phobia will result. It is not unusual for the onset of such school refusal to take place after the child has been kept home because of an actual physical illness or, even without that, after a long weekend. That seems to suggest that the pleasant experiences associated with being at home have made home appear more attractive than school or, to put it another way, to have reinforced being home. If being home breeds staying home, the importance of early return to school can be readily understood.

Even in cases where the child has encountered an event at school that was associated with experiencing fear, the importance of an early return to school cannot be overstressed. The old notion of getting right back on the horse after having fallen off has a great deal of merit because it is psychologically sound. Sitting on a horse and falling off is a complex situation. Falling off is fear arousing, and the person who has this experience is likely to attach the fear to the situation in which it was first experienced: the sitting on the horse and, by generalization, to the horse and other horses.

A PARADOX

Fears, presumably, are maintained by repeated exposure to the fear-arousing situation, and they are expected to diminish (extinguish) when this situation is never again encountered.

In order to lose one's fear of falling off horses and one's fear of horses, one must have the experience of sitting on the horse without falling off. One must, in other words, experience the feared situation in the absence of the experience which aroused the fear. That is, unfortunately, what the person with a horse phobia is not able to experience, because the avoidance of horses keeps such a person from the experience necessary for extinguishing the fear. Yet, since this person is also not reexperiencing the original fear-producing condition, what is it that maintains (reinforces) the fear?

Most psychologists believe that the answer to this paradox lies in the fact that fears have both physiological and psychological components and that each component may be capable of eliciting the other. So, if thinking about falling off a horse can get one's adrenalin to flow, or if the flow of adrenalin is greater in the presence of a horse than it is in response to some other circumstance, a person may very well attribute these feelings of arousal to fears of horses. Since fear is an unpleasant state that we are motivated to terminate as soon as possible, the quickest way of doing so is by avoiding horses, even to the point of not thinking about them. This avoidance response is now rewarded (reinforced) by the reduction of the unpleasant fear. So that each time one experiences a reduction of fear by avoiding horses, one will learn to maintain this behavior pattern. Thus, by not getting back on the horse and permitting oneself to experience not falling off, the fear itself cannot undergo extinction and may be maintained for a lifetime, ready to reemerge at the slightest thought of a horse.

Let us now substitute "school" for "horse" in this reasoning. What the child needs at the earliest possible moment after first encountering a fear-arousing event in school is to return to school so that he or she can experience the school situation without the fear-arousing event. This should lead to the fear becoming extinguished, particularly if the child can encounter some pleasant events and is rewarded (reinforced) for going to school. If, on the other hand, the child is allowed to remain at home, the very thought of school will reawaken the fear which, when reduced by not going to school, reinforces the school avoidance. The longer this goes on, the more ingrained the fear will become and the more difficult it will be ultimately to get the child to return to school. Add to this the reinforcement the child receives for staying home by experiencing all the pleasant things that go on around the home, like watching television and eating mother's food. Moreover, the negative aspects of school will increase as a result of being estranged from classmates, and if the child has fallen very far behind in his school work, one can see why returning there becomes more and more of a problem.

VALERIE, MOTHER, AND SCHOOL

Valerie had attended kindergarten and first grade without difficulty. In the second grade she began skipping school from time to time and had a total of 41 absences during that year. She threw violent temper tantrums, screamed, and cried so that her mother found it nearly impossible to get her out of the house. After four days of attending, Valerie ceased to go to school entirely.

Her mother took eight-year-old Val to a school counselor, physician, and a social worker, all of whom gave extensive advice. One said, "Ignore the behavior and it will go away." Another suggested that Mother give Valerie plenty of praise and affection, while a third recommended that she be punished severely if she refused to go to school. Dutifully following each of these recommendations in turn,

Val's mother found that none had the desired result. Following a psychological evaluation at the pediatric clinic of the local hospital, the mother was advised that Valerie's difficulties were such that she would require long-term psychiatric treatment. The cost of such treatment was beyond the means of this low-income family, and the mother decided that she would just have to learn to live with the problem.

This, fortunately, is not the end of the story. A psychologist from the nearby university happened to hear about this case and recommended trying a behavioral approach, based on the psychological principle (discussed in Chapter 7) that behavior is a function of its consequences. Careful observations quickly revealed that the consequences Valerie experienced for not going to school were to be permitted to sleep late and to have time alone with her mother after her sister and brothers had gone to school. When it was time for Mother to go to work, Valerie would be taken to a neighbor's apartment where she was free to do whatever she pleased for the rest of the day.

The behavioral management program which was now instituted began with having Helen, a female assistant, join Val at the neighbor's house and involve her in academically related work, such as using arithmetic flash cards. Val showed neither panic, fear, or any other disturbance. In fact she appeared to enjoy the work. After two days of this activity, the two, after completing the academic work, went together for a ride in Helen's car.

Next came the crucial step. Having been assured the singular support of the principal and the classroom teacher, the decision was made to have Val and Helen go to the school toward the end of the school day. Though Val's eyes widened when she was told of this plan, she offered no resistance and, holding hands, she and Helen entered the classroom together. With Helen sitting nearby, Val was given some classroom material, and she immediately started doing some schoolwork. Over the next six days, Val was taken to school a little earlier each day and Helen stayed in the classroom a little less of the time. Now came a setback. When Helen stopped taking Val, the child once again refused to go to school.

At this point, a home-based motivational system, which involved the mother's direct participation, was instituted. For the next nine days, Mother would take Valerie to school. Instead of kicking and screaming, as she had done in the past, the girl now went without difficulty, probably because going to school and spending the day there had now been made the occasion for earning explicit praise and a special reward in the evening. Nonetheless, Val still would not go to school on her own. So the psychologists modified the procedure once more. The mother was to leave the house before it was time for the children to go to school. Mother would go to the school first, wait there for the children, and reward them when they showed up.

This worked for one day. On the following day the sister and brothers arrived at the school, but no Valerie. As arranged, Mother walked back to the house, picked up Valerie, and brought her to school. Since school was about a mile's walk from home, these round trips were a considerable inconvenience for Mother. Needless to say, when Mother came after Valerie, she was not exactly pleased with her daughter and clearly expressed her annoyance. Staying home was no longer rewarded as it once had been. On the other hand, attending school did earn rewards, such as the privilege of having a favorite cousin stay overnight at the house.

After ten days of having Mother wait for the children at school (on only two of which she had to go back home for Valerie), this aspect of the procedure was dropped, though the rewards were continued for another month. Valerie continued to attend school without difficulty.

The entire intervention procedure had taken forty-five days! While Valerie had previously been an average C student, she now earned A's and B's, voluntarily assisted the teacher with small errands, and was chosen as school guide for a new student. Where she once had been "quiet as a mouse" in class, without friends, and unhappy, Valerie was now invited to join the Brownie Scout group and seemed genuinely fond of school. She had maintained a perfect attendance record when an inquiry was made nine months after she had returned to school and she lived, we hope, happily ever after!

Based on a report by T. Ayllon, D. Smith, and M. Rogers entitled, "Behavioral management of school phobia," and published in *Behavior Therapy and Experimental Psychiatry,* 1970, vol. 1, pp. 125–138.

EARLY INTERVENTION

One of the first to recognize the implications of the formulation that fear feeds on itself and to translate his recognition into action designed to help young children at the incipient stages of school phobia was Dr. Wallace Kennedy, at Florida State University. His approach to children in the early years of school for whom school refusal is the first such episode is to insist on immediate intervention. In order to have this program function well, one must have good professional relations with the school system so that cases of school refusal will be immediately referred for help. Physicians must cooperate so that no unnecessary medical excuses for school absence will be given and, most important of all, the parents must be willing to take a major responsibility for the intervention.

In this approach, the child and his parents are given interviews as soon as possible after onset of the problem. The child, who must be seen after school hours to emphasize that *nothing* is more important than going to school, is told why it is important to face one's fears directly. The parents are given assurance that every day that the child remains out of school will make his fears worse and that school attendance must be enforced if the problem is to be solved. The parents are instructed not to enter into lengthy discussions with the child regarding school attendance or the "problem." The night before, the child is to be told, "Tomorrow you go back to school" and this plan is followed the next day in a matter-of-fact way. The child should not be asked how he feels, or why he is afraid of school, or why he doesn't like school. One parent, usually the father, is to take the child to school, turn him over to school personnel, and leave. That evening, the child is to be complimented on going to school and staying there, no matter how stormy that attendance may have been. Progress is recognized, no matter how minimal. If the child has been at school for thirty minutes, that is progress and he is told that the next day will be much better. Beyond that, nothing is said about school and the next morning the procedure is repeated, with more praise and compliments that evening. By the third day, the child should be virtually without problems. By that evening the family can celebrate his success at overcoming his difficulty with considerable fanfare, and possibly a party in his honor.

The Kennedy procedure may seem brutal to some, but it is based on the recognition that the child is harmed more in the long run by not attending school than by suffering the indignity of being carried into the school by a parent. What is more, Kennedy reported that this method was successful with every one of the sixty cases with whom he used this approach in that the children not only returned to school and remained there, but that a follow-up over as long as twelve years later revealed neither a repetition of school refusal nor a substitution of other psychological problems.

If one insists that a child return to school despite his or her fears, one does, of course, shoulder a heavy responsibility. The indication is that there is indeed no realistic basis for the child's fears. Should it be the case that there is a bully at school who has threatened to hurt the child, or if the teacher makes unreasonable demands of the child or threatens some dire punishment for poor work, it would be grossly unwise and potentially dangerous to force the child to return to this realistically fear-arousing situation. A careful investigation of what is going on in school (or on the way to and from school) must be an integral part of the kind of treatment advocated by Kennedy. It may be, in fact, that Kennedy's success was related to his clinic's excellent and open communications with the schools, so that he had a fairly good idea of the type of setting with which he was working. Furthermore, the families of the school-phobic children with whom his treatment worked so remarkably well were described as maintaining open communication and as having good relationships. It is in such families that parents not only know what kind of school their child is attending, but the communication pattern at home is such that the child can freely verbalize concerns about untoward conditions in the school. The parent can then intervene long before the child's fears come to a head in full-blown school refusal.

We have been talking about school refusal in younger children for whom the episode is the first and where the onset is recent. What about older children and adolescents who refuse to go to school? What about children who have a long history of school refusal or who have been staying away from school for a long time? Here the problem is far more serious and the chances for bringing about a reversal are less favorable. Often such refusal to attend school is but one of many psychological and behavior problems manifested by these youngsters. One often finds severe conflicts with parents and other signs of family disorganization, antisocial behavior, and trouble with authority. It is likely that here we are not dealing with school phobia in the sense of a disabling fear of school, but with situations where refusal to go to school is merely one expression of refusing all kinds of other things the adult world expects and demands. In these instances a far-reaching change in environment, such as removal from the home and a move to a residential school, may often be the best way of resolving the conflicts.

OTHER FORMS OF MANAGING SCHOOL PHOBIAS

As we have said earlier, the longer a child is permitted to remain away from school, the more difficult it becomes to get attendance resumed. This is probably one of the reasons why protracted psychotherapy, ostensibly designed to uncover a presumed "underlying problem," is generally ineffectual. Not only does the child continue to miss school, falling further and further behind in the work and getting all the positive reinforcements which staying at home brings with it, but the therapist's focus on the child's problems, the interest and concern demonstrated, with the special attention inevitably entailed, all appear to be counterproductive from the point of view of getting the child back to school.

Yet, there are instances where the chance to use Kennedy's approach was missed during the first few days of school refusal or where the child's expressed fears are so great that no one has the stomach to force a return to school. In these instances a more gradual return to school can be tried. This entails a modified form of desensitization to the feared object.

Fear of school can be graded from its highest intensity, which is elicited by being in the school itself, to its lowest intensity, which might be talking about school or seeing a picture of the school building. A therapist can help the child approach the school by a series of graded steps. In one such intervention, the therapist and the child approached the school together, first sitting in a car in front of the school until this situation ceased to elicit fear, then eventually entering the empty classroom for a brief period of time, until, at the end, the child was able to tolerate being in the class together with the teacher and other students. In this manner, the fear appears to be gradually diminished while approaching the feared situation is repeatedly rewarded by the therapist's approval and encouragement. It goes without saying that here, as in similar methods, the understanding cooperation of the school authorities and the classroom teacher are essential.

Separation Anxiety. We said at the beginning of this chapter that school refusal can take three forms: truancy, school phobia, and separation anxiety. The process of going to school has a beginning and an end, with many steps in between. The school-phobic child's problem lies at the end of this process; the feared situation is being in the classroom, or being called on to recite, or taking a test. At the other end of this chain lies leaving the home and the people (usually the mother) in it. If a child fears leaving the mother for some reason or other, the effect is that he is not going to school, but since the fear is not associated with the school, this problem should not be called a school phobia. Separation anxiety is a more apt description.

In these cases it is necessary to ascertain what there is about leaving the mother that makes it so unpleasant. Is it that the mother does so many nice things for the child that leaving her is equated with losing these opportunities? Is it that being away from mother entails not being able to watch that she doesn't get hurt or doesn't give jealously treasured attention to a little brother or sister? It is these issues which must be dealt with if the child is to feel comfortable about leaving the home to go to school. A gradual "weaning" from the mother, somewhat analogous to the gradual desensitization of fear of school, is often a good way of dealing with this problem.

Separation anxiety is often as much related to the mother's reluctance to have the child leave her as it is to the child's fear of leaving the mother. Mother and child thus support each other's clinging together and each must learn to let go. As the child gradually discovers that leaving the mother is not fraught with danger, the mother must learn that her existence as a woman does not depend on having the child in constant contact with her—that, in fact, she is doing more for the child in

permitting him or her to begin having an independent existence than in encouraging and supporting a dependent
clinging.

The methods therapists might use to deal with a separation
anxiety will vary, depending on their orientation. As usual, the
most immediate effect is obtained by those who deal with the
problem at the level of behavior, those who look at what the
mother does and what the child does and seek to modify these
actions. By beginning their intervention a step at a time, having
the child leave mother for relatively brief periods and then
returning and making sure that during these periods both
mother and child experience something positive and anxiety
reducing, such behavior therapists often succeed in lengthen-
ing these separation periods fairly soon so that the child is able
to stay away from mother long enough to begin to attend
school. Other therapists may prefer to explore with both mother
and child what they imagine might happen as a result of their
separating. The therapist would try, with the mother and child,
to ascertain how these fantasies arose and what they might
mean. Even where this approach succeeds, its lengthy course
will have the effect of prolonging the time during which mother
and child remain inseparable, and in a young child's life every
week that is lost from learning to interact with other children or
from going to school represents a delay in the vital process of
growing up.

Lesson Refusal

One cannot leave the topic of school refusal without recognizing
that a refusal to attend school is not the only way in which a
child can respond to unpleasant school-related experiences,
particularly where these experiences have to do with such specifics as doing the work demanded by the teacher or responding
to teacher's questions. In these instances, what the child is
avoiding is not going to school but participating in the activities
demanded by the school personnel. Here we are dealing not
with fear of school, as was the case with school phobia, but with
the effects of many unrewarding experiences related to participating in classroom activities. Lesson refusal might be a term by

which to identify this behavior. Such a child might be described as not paying attention, as daydreaming, as restless, or as simply "doing nothing."

These words have also been used in connection with learning-disabled children, but here we are faced with a different set of circumstances. These can best be viewed in terms of the consequences of reward, nonreward, and punishment. We know that behavior that is rewarded (reinforced) is very likely to be repeated, while behavior that is not rewarded or punished tends to appear less and less frequently until it is finally no longer to be observed. If one now construes active participation in ongoing classroom activities ("paying attention") as a complex combination of behaviors, we can ask what will happen to this behavior under rewarding, nonrewarding, and punishing conditions.

Rewards. Rewards can take many forms and what is rewarding to one child need not necessarily be rewarding to another. In fact, the technical definition of positive reinforcement (reward) states that it is any event which, when taking place as a consequence of a given behavior, will make that behavior more likely to occur when similar conditions are once again present. It seems that intrinsically neutral events, such as a teacher's nod, can acquire reinforcing qualities. As a result, some children are reinforced by a teacher's nod, others by a teacher's smile, others by a teacher's words of praise. Simply receiving the teacher's attention, regardless of the content of this attention, appears to be a powerful reinforcing event for many children.

With this in mind, one can say that a child who pays attention and encounters a reinforcing consequence is a child who should continue to pay attention in the future. On the other hand, a child who does not encounter a reinforcing event in consequence of class participation may gradually cease attending to the ongoing work.

Not being reinforced for paying attention can result from two conditions. One is that the teacher does not provide this child with any of the potentially reinforcing experiences. The other is that the consequences the teacher does make available do not have reinforcing value for that child. In the first instance, the teacher, who takes paying attention on the part of children for granted, ignores those who are doing what they are expected to do, often giving a great deal of attention to those who are engaging in undesirable behavior. In the second instance, the teacher may be nodding at, smiling to, or praising a child but, for that child, these events do not possess a reinforcing quality. As we said, these events must have acquired reinforcing quality before they can have an effect, and in the case of that particular child this development has never taken place. We can speculate about the conditions where a child might fail to learn that a praise statement coming from a teacher is a "good thing," but that would not be very constructive. More to the point is to ask what one can do when one wishes to reward a child for whom the usual rewards are meaningless. Various privileges, more directly physical consequences such as a pat on the back or a stroke of the hair, or rather concrete rewards, such as marks on a paper, tokens, or prizes, are often effective in classes where the more abstract and verbal rewards are ineffective. We shall have more to say about these matters in the next chapter.

Whether a child sits in class paying attention or doing nothing can often be a function of the consequences he or she has encountered. True, many children immerse themselves in schoolwork despite the fact that the teacher rarely if ever praises them or otherwise presents a reward. These are children for whom doing well in school has in itself acquired reward value, probably because there is some reward for doing well available at home. We are not here concerned with those children but with those who have failed to bring this motivational structure to school and for whom some special effort on the part of the teacher is essential.

Punishment. So far we have spoken of reward and nonreward. Let us look at the third alternative, punishment. While the image that immediately comes to mind when one sees the word punishment is some physical form of inflicting pain, punishment takes many forms and again it is best to look at the technical definition of that term. Punishment is any event which, appearing as a consequence of a given behavior, makes that behavior less likely to appear when similar circumstances are present in the future. Following that definition, a teacher's smile might be a punishment. If a child were to look at the teacher and each time that happened the teacher smiled at the child, and if we were to observe that the child's looking at the teacher became less and less frequent, we would have to conclude that the teacher's smile is, for that child, a punishment. Strange? Not at all. Were the child able to put the events into words, he might well say, "I can't stand it when she grins at me!" Conceivable. The point is, what is rewarding to one can be punishing for another and vice versa. For some children being yelled at by the teacher can actually be a form of positive reinforcement ("I get a kick out of seeing her get mad").

These are the more unusual circumstances, but we must, nonetheless, keep them in mind. The more likely circumstance is that children view such events as reprimands, admonitions, and scoldings as negative consequences, to say nothing of the still all too frequent practice of physical punishment. The child who is frequently punished for "not paying attention" is not likely to learn paying attention (only positive reinforcement can do that). What such children are likely to learn is to look as if they were paying attention (to avoid punishment) or to fight back in a more or less direct manner. It is here where the defiant, annoying, impudent, verbally abusive, and, at times, openly assaultive student may be created. That anger at constantly punishing adults can also find expression in the destruction of the property associated with these adults (vandalism of school property) should not be too surprising.

Chapter 9

THE CHILD WHOSE BEHAVIOR IS A SOURCE OF TROUBLE

We have been dealing with children who have trouble learning or who refuse to go to school. We turn now to the child whose behavior results in frequent complaints by the school authorities. Such a child gets into trouble either because of fighting with other children or because of classroom behavior which the teacher considers unacceptable. This may take the form of talking out of turn, not remaining seated, or arguing with the teacher. Since these behaviors tend to disrupt school decorum, such children are often referred to as disruptive children, though words like aggressive, negativistic, sassy, unruly, or undisciplined can also be heard in this context.

The Aggressive Child

Aggression is, no doubt, the most vexing problem with which our society is trying to deal. Whether it be in the form of aggression on the part of nations who engage in armed conflict, aggression on the part of political groups perpetrating acts of violence, aggression on the part of urban gangs fighting one another, aggression on the part of individuals committing crimes of violence, or aggression on the part of one child beating up another, we are constantly faced with the question how best to deal with aggression so as to reduce or control it. Not too surprisingly, theories of aggression abound and the verbal strife between the proponents of the various theories often takes on rather aggressive dimensions. There are those who hold that aggression is a natural attribute of the human species, an instinct as it were, that helped us in the struggle of primitive survival and thus became a part of our evolutionary heritage. From that point of view, aggression is here to stay, and we must, therefore, learn to live with it by working out means of channeling and controlling this instinct. Others would maintain that there is nothing "natural" about aggression, that it is instead a maladaptive response to conditions, such as crowded urban living or economic scarcity, which mankind has created and must rectify if aggression is to be eliminated.

Whether one views aggression as a natural instinct or as a pathological response to abnormal conditions has a lot to do with one's basic convictions about the nature of humanity. Are we inherently good or bad by nature? These are philosophical questions relating to the nature of evil, the expulsion from Paradise, the slaying of Abel, and original sin. The psychologist has no answer to these questions, but when psychologists turn to the study of aggression, they are immediately faced with an unexpected problem.

What Is Aggression? One would think that aggression is a word that does not need to be defined before it can be used; everybody knows what we mean by aggression. Or do they? The 1974 edition of *Webster's New Collegiate Dictionary* speaks of "a forceful action or procedure (as an unprovoked attack) especially when intended to dominate or master" and of "hostile, injurious, or destructive behavior or outlook especially when caused by frustration." For a psychologist looking for an objective definition of aggression so that it might be studied, these definitions raise more questions than they answer. How much force is needed before an action is declared forceful? From whose point of view must an attack be unprovoked in order to qualify as aggression? How do we know that the person who engages in the action "intends" to dominate or master? Is hostile behavior and a hostile outlook the same thing, or should one not differentiate between an aggressive act and an aggressive attitude? How does one know when an act is caused by frustration and, for that matter, what do we mean by "frustration"? Could it be that aggression cannot be objectively defined but lies, like beauty, in the eye of the beholder?

There are many ways of approaching the study of aggression from the standpoint of a psychologist. It can be viewed as a characteristic of the species, as an emotion, as a motivation, as an attitude, or as a response. The formulation of aggression as a response has thus far been the most fruitful in terms of generating testable hypotheses. Therefore, we shall examine this formulation for, as we shall see, it lends itself well to an understanding of aggression in children and can lead to better ways of coping with it.

Aggression Is a Response.   Aggression is a response, a response that the person at whom it is directed considers noxious, unpleasant, and unwanted. It is a response from which the recipient (for whom it is a stimulus) would just as soon escape. Aggression is an interpersonal act, something that involves an agent and a recipient, and we can designate the act as aggressive only if we know its effect on the recipient. Regardless of the intention of the agent ("I didn't mean to hurt him"), an action may be defined as aggressive if the recipient doesn't like it and if the recipient views it as such. This is what we had in mind when we said aggression lies in the eye of the beholder. The question to be asked, therefore, is not whether a person is angry, frustrated, or intending to be aggressive; the question must concern itself with the effect of the act. The smothering embrace of an effusive maiden aunt when intrusively imposed on (forced upon!) a reluctant child can become an act of aggression. The child would just as soon avoid the experience. Aggression thus entails the delivery of an aversive stimulus to another person. As in the case of positive reinforcement and punishment (see Chapter 8), the definition of aggression depends on the effect of the event.

An aversive stimulus can take a variety of forms; hence, aggression takes a variety of forms. It can involve the infliction of physical pain, the damaging of someone's property, the withholding of earned rewards, the presentation of such irritating stimuli as loud noises, bright lights, or noxious fumes, keeping someone from reaching a desired goal, or presenting someone with negative evaluations ("name calling").

Now we don't always call every one of these events instances of aggression. Pain inflicted in the course of medical or dental treatment, parents keeping a child from ingesting a marble, or telling students that they have failed an examination are not considered acts of aggression. Furthermore, what is an irritating loud noise to one may be music to the ears of another. If the radio happens to be played in the presence of both these people, is the owner of the instrument aggressive? Lastly, calling someone a fool may, under certain circumstances, be a term of endearment.

All of these examples indicate that there is no absolute definition of aggression. A given response is labeled aggression under one set of circumstances, but under different circumstances it may be given a different label, even though the recipient deems the experience aversive. Take, for example, the case of the patient in the chair of a dentist. Clearly the pain which the dentist (unintentionally) inflicts on the patient is a noxious stimulus which the patient would just as soon avoid, but neither patient, nor dentist, nor a third person looking on would call the dentist's behavior aggressive. So, we have arrived at the notion that aggression is aggression when we call it aggression. In other words, the definition of aggression is a matter of consensus, of social convention. What is rambunctious horseplay in one neighborhood is the intolerable aggressive acting out of a bunch of hoodlum kids in another.

On the whole, a response is likely to be labeled as aggressive (because the recipient may seek to avoid it) when it is of high magnitude or intensity. The hardness of pressure makes for the difference between a squeeze and a pinch; the velocity of hand movement differentiates the pat on the cheek from the slap in the face; the force of the arm movement determines whether the cuff on the shoulder is a friendly gesture or a hostile attack.

The capacity for emitting high-magnitude responses is clearly a biological given. The occasions when we emit such a response appears subject to learning. Under what conditions are we apt to learn to emit responses of high magnitude which, because they annoy, irritate, or hurt other people, are likely to be called aggressive?

Since we have defined aggression as a response and are now asking about ways in which this response can be learned, we should look for situations where the response has a high probability of being reinforced. The most likely of such situations is when we want something, like another child's toy, and we obtain it as the consequence of making a forceful response like pushing, hitting, kicking, or screaming. It is less likely, unfortunately, that a mild, polite, low-intensity response will lead to the desired goal and thus to reinforcement than it is for one of these high-magnitude, aggressive responses to achieve gratification.

In theory, it should be possible to raise a totally unaggressive child by almost always rewarding low magnitude requests and never rewarding high-magnitude demands, by teaching the child that goals can be reached by peaceful means. Maybe that is impossible. Stuck doors do open when we pull hard, balky candy machines do deliver when we kick them, people do get out of our way when we shove, and others do give up their possessions when we grab. In each of these instances we are reinforced for making high-magnitude responses which, in the last two examples, are probably labeled as aggressive.

The world in which we live is more likely to provide payoff for high-magnitude, aggressive responses than for responses, such as polite requests, that do not fall in the category of aggression. In addition to the external situations which tend to favor the development of aggressive responses, there is also an internal state that further conspires to strengthen the chances for aggressive responses to occur when we find ourselves blocked from access to a desired goal. Situations where we are so blocked are situations entailing frustration. Despite the fact that the word frustration is often used as if it were an emotion ("I feel frustrated"), it is best to limit the use of this term to describing environmental situations. Thus, we shall refer to a situation where access to a goal is blocked by someone or something as a frustration situation. This makes frustration a stimulus. Since we have already decided to view aggression as a response, we can now speak of aggression as the response we learn to make to the stimulus situation of frustration because the consequences of getting to our goal (removing the frustrating condition) reinforces that response. But what about the internal state we mentioned?

Anger and Aggression. A situation where a goal is blocked elicits a physiological arousal state, apparently involving certain biochemical changes which facilitate and sustain a higher level of activity, that is to say, a higher magnitude of responses. The presence of this arousal state can be demonstrated by sensitive measuring devices which will show both electrical and chemical changes. It probably served the survival of our species, thus representing the product of evolutionary pressures. When we experience this arousal state under conditions of frustration, we give it a name; we call it anger. It may be that the same or a very similar arousal state experienced under different conditions is given a different name, such as excitement, elation, or fear, but this issue need not concern us here. For our purposes we need only to consider the formulation that frustration elicits anger. Anger is an unpleasant sensation and the removal of an unpleasant sensation is another way of reinforcing a response. This is what psychologists call negative reinforcement (which is quite different from punishment, incidentally). If one finds oneself faced with an unpleasant state of affairs and one makes a response that terminates that state of affairs, the response which had that effect tends to be learned. That is, the next time a similar state of affairs obtains, the previously reinforced response is likely to be repeated.

Now it so happens that if frustration elicits anger and if a high-magnitude response (which is probably facilitated by the arousal) removes the frustration, then this high-magnitude response will be reinforced not only by obtaining the goal but also by reduction of anger. Since, as we have already shown, high-magnitude responses tend to be labeled as aggressive, aggression has two sources of reinforcement: positive reinforcement from reaching the goal and negative reinforcement from reducing the anger. It may be that the high incidence of aggression and the difficulty we encounter in seeking to limit and reduce it are a function of this double source of reinforcement.

Since the situation we label frustration is such a favorable condition for learning aggressive responses, it is not surprising that psychologists thought for a long time that frustration and aggression are inevitably linked. That this is not the case can be demonstrated in two ways. One is by teaching children to cope with frustrating situations by other than aggressive, that is, by constructive means. The other is by allusion to the many situations where people engage in behavior we would all label as acts of aggression but where they encounter neither frustration nor anger, that is, when they aggress against others "in cold blood."

Aggression Can Be Learned. Thus far we have spoken of reinforcement of aggression as coming from two sources: goal attainment and anger reduction. There are, however, at least two more ways through which children (and adults) can learn to make aggressive responses. One is by having meaningful adults who are sources of important reinforcers such as food, affection, approval, attention, or desired objects, present such reinforcement upon occasions where either the child or someone else is engaging in aggressive behavior. How would that be done? One way, of course, is for the adult to see to it that the child gets what she wants when she is emitting aggressive responses. A younger child is trying to pull a toy away from an older sibling. He is in rage and screaming and yelling, but the older one is holding her ground. Now the mother, irritated by the noise, tells the older child, "Give it to him already" and the older child obeys. Aggression has paid off and both children have learned a lesson. The younger has been directly reinforced and the older had a free demonstration of the success of aggression.

Parental approval is another source of reinforcement. If a child is engaging in aggressive behavior and the parent stands by either overtly approving or failing to disapprove (which children usually interpret as tacit approval), aggression is also reinforced. Consider, too, the effect of the child on observing a parent approvingly watch a boxing match or a rough hockey game on television.

We can next turn to the effect of a parent as a model. It is now well established that a great deal of learning takes place through observation of others even when we ourselves are not actually engaging in the behavior being learned. The older child who, in the earlier example, observed the younger child being reinforced for aggression was learning through modeling. It would have to be predicted that next time that child found herself in a frustrating situation she would be more likely than before to attempt resolving that situation in an aggressive way. In fact, this has been demonstrated in a long-term observation study of nursery school children which showed that when aggression "pays off," aggressive children become more aggressive and initially passive children learn to be aggressive. While other children are important models, adults, because of their position of relative power and their control over important reinforcers, are even more potent models. Thus, when a child observes a parent engaging in aggression and thereby obtaining reinforcement, the child is likely to learn making similar responses in similar situations. The most potent of such modeling situations is the one where a parent is meting out physical punishment to a child.

Aggression and Punishment. For those who believe that physical punishment can serve to eliminate undesirable behavior, the well-documented observation that parents who punish the aggressive behavior of their children raise highly aggressive children may seem like a paradox. A behavioral theory of social learning, however, predicts exactly that outcome.

It is true that infliction of pain immediately following a given behavior will suppress that behavior under similar circumstances on future occasions. The key words in this phrase are *under similar circumstances.* If an aggressive act, such as kicking little brother, took place at home and in the presence of a parent and the parent, in turn, hit the perpetrator, it is likely that little brother will not be kicked again in the home and in the presence of the parent. On the other hand, it is not unlikely that next time a kicking response will be aimed at a neighbor child, away from the home, and out of sight of the parent. Punishment, it seems, does not eliminate a response, it only changes the occasions when that response is emitted.

Another attribute of punishment which makes it an inefficient method of changing behavior is the delay that usually transpires between the commission of the act and the receipt of punishment. Like reward, punishment loses its potency when there is such a delay. Since many transgressions are not observed firsthand by the punishing agent and, often, don't become apparent until an informer reports or the evidence is found, punishment may come to be associated not with the prohibited act but with the occasion of father coming home or with dinner table conversation when little brother tattles.

Modeling, however, is probably the most important reason why aggressive children have punitive parents and vice versa. We said earlier that a great deal can be learned from observing someone else engaging in a given behavior. What does the child observe when a parent engages in punishment? The child sees that when one is angry one hits someone who is smaller and weaker. If the child is the one being hit, it is also likely that the child is emotionally aroused (afraid) and a state of such arousal appears to enhance learning. We thus have a situation where the lesson has an excellent chance of being learned. Is it then any wonder that a child who has many such experiences will acquire the behavior pattern that will lead to aggressive behavior directed at smaller and weaker children whenever that child's anger is aroused by having another block access to a desired goal?

"Get It Out of Your System." When one views behavior and emotions as if they were a hydraulic system of pressures and safety valves, one may develop the idea that aggression can be "drained off" by channeling it into safe, socially acceptable outlets. Many parents, gym teachers, and child psychotherapists hold to this notion. As a result, they advocate vigorous (aggressive) activity in play, sports, and therapy sessions on the assumption that this will permit children to get aggressive impulses out of their system, thus reducing their aggression in areas where it is inappropriate. There is, unfortunately, no scientific basis for this catharsis approach to aggression. Human behavior is not the product of a steam kettle that must have an opening lest it explode. In fact, aggression, like other behavior, can be expected to occur more rather than less frequently when it is given expression under conditions where it has positive consequences.

It can and has been demonstrated that when high-magnitude responses, such as those we label as aggressive, are reinforced by adult praise, approval, or even mere permissiveness, these responses will be more likely to occur at a later time. For example, if one trains boys to engage in high-velocity hitting of a punching-bag doll by rewarding them for such hitting and then lets these boys play with another child in a competitive game, it can be shown that these boys will engage in more kicking, punching, pulling, and pushing than a group who had previously been trained to make low-velocity responses. Aggressionlike games thus do not reduce the likelihood of later personal aggression; on the contrary, they seem to increase it.

There is also evidence that when a permissive adult encourages a child to make aggressive statements about another person, it will increase the chances that this child will later behave aggressively toward that person. Furthermore, when one gives a child who is angry at another child an opportunity to engage in aggression toward a substitute target (such as a picture of the victim), the effect will be that more rather than less aggression will ultimately be directed at that victim.

All of this, of course, relates to the much debated issue of the effect of viewing violence on television. Those who subscribe to the hydraulic model of aggression have advocated the notion that potential aggression can be "drained off" vicariously by watching others engage in aggression. This should make the boxing fan one of our most peaceful citizens, and children who watch a lot of television programs with violent content should become a generation of pacifists. That this is not the case has now been repeatedly demonstrated, and the fact that the opposite is true has, fortunately, begun to influence the content of television programs aimed at children.

Can One Raise a Nonaggressive Child? We can now venture a prescription for raising children who are not aggressive if that is one's goal in child rearing. The parent should, first of all, neither approve, condone, nor model aggressive behavior. That means that whenever aggression is encountered, whether emitted by the child or by someone else, the parent must indicate disapproval. It also means that the parent should not resort to direct aggression as a form of punishment. This does not mean that punishment should never be used, but there are punishments, such as deprivation of privileges, including the privilege of playing with other children, and verbal reprimand, which do not involve the infliction of physical pain.

An extremely important corollary to no approving or modeling aggression is to teach the child nonagressive constructive alternatives to coping with situations where aggression has taken place. Responses that are incompatible with aggression should be strengthened by rewarding them, ideally by giving the child access to the goal, the blocking of which would otherwise lead to aggression. This does not mean that the child should always be given his or her own way; extreme indulgence is just as unrealistic and harmful as extreme deprivation. There are all kinds of ways of letting a child reach a desired goal, and these ways can teach nonaggressive, socially constructive behavior. Many will involve a delay of gratification—taking turns, sharing a toy, or saving toward the eventual acquisition of a desired object.

It will be apparent that all of what has been said entails parental decisions and parental values. We have assumed that a parent decries aggressive behavior in children and considers sharing and taking turns a desirable form of social interaction. The question obviously arises whether a child who is raised so as to be nonaggressive will be able to cope with the demands of the world that will be encountered outside the home. Some may say that pacifism entails paying a price; others may feel that nonaggression has its limits and that one should fight for one's rights, or defend oneself when attacked. All parents must answer these questions in terms of their own value system and in accordance with their ideas about what kind of a person they want their child to become. Psychology can only present methods for accomplishing certain goals; it cannot set these goals.

The Management of Classroom Problems

There is a logical consequence of looking at behavior not as something that hovers within a child and must have an outlet, but as something that is acquired under specifiable conditions as a function of what followed the behavior. That is, in order to change a child's behavior we don't take him or her into the privacy of a psychologist's consulting room, there to explore the child's "inner workings," but we examine the situation where the child's objectionable behavior takes place and seek to influence that behavior in that situation. Thus, if a child's behavior disrupts the activities of the classroom, one must examine what goes on in the classroom immediately before and just after the objectionable behavior occurs and, having specified these conditions, seek to change them, thereby changing the disruptive child's behavior.

This behavioral orientation is, of course, quite different from traditional views of child behavior where what a child does in class is attributed to something going on inside the child, rather than to something going on in the classroom. One used to speak of a child as being emotionally disturbed, minimally brain damaged, or mentally ill, words which attribute the problem to things the child carries around from place to place. The fact that many children who are a source of complaint in school are quite unremarkable at home and other settings clearly contradicts the assumption of this steady-state theory of behavior. We shall here operate on the assumption that behavior is situation specific, and we shall explore the implications of this view for helping children whom the school describes as disruptive.

In Chapter 7 we discussed the principles of behavior according to which positive consequences of a given action strengthen that action, while negative consequences or an absence of consequences weaken that action. Strengthening and weakening of an action are reflected in an increase or a decrease in the likelihood of that action being repeated at a later time. As we said earlier, behavior is a function of its consequences. There is another part of this relationship between action and consequence, however, and that is the situation in which action and consequence are encountered. If an action takes place in a given situation or context and is followed by a reinforcing consequence, then the theory of behavior would predict that this action is likely to be repeated *when the same context is again present.* If, in a different situation, the same action was not reinforced, one would not expect that action to recur in that situation.

In more technical terms, what we are here talking about is the predictable relationship between stimulus condition (situa-

tion), response (action), and reinforcement (positive consequence), which was postulated by B. F. Skinner of Harvard and
which has been repeatedly confirmed both in experiments and
applications.

What One Can Learn in School. Let us see how this principle
can help us understand why a child who is "perfectly well
behaved" at home can be a hellion at school or vice versa.
Clearly, home and school represent distinctly different stimulus
conditions, and such a child has apparently learned to behave
in one way at home and in another way at school. The question
which immediately comes to mind is, "Why?" but that is the
wrong question. If the answer we are seeking is to be scientific
rather than philosophical, the question we must ask is, "How?"
Under what circumstances will a child learn one kind of behavior in one setting and a different kind of behavior in another?

If we were able to make careful and detailed observations,
we would probably find that the same behavior has one kind of
consequence in school and quite a different kind of consequence at home. If, for example, "hellion" behavior pays off in
school but is ignored at home, while "good behavior" is
rewarded at home but ignored at school, our principles would
predict that the child would behave quite differently in the two
settings. The "payoff" we are talking about often comes from a
rather unlikely consequence: teachers' reprimands.

Careful observation of what goes on in the typical classroom demonstrates the following. Quiet, task oriented, "good"
behavior is by and large ignored, while inattentive, disruptive,
"bad" behavior is again and again followed by teacher's attention in the form of reprimands or other intervention. Since such
observations also demonstrate that the "bad" behavior does not
decrease in frequency but, on the contrary, occurs more often
over time, we must conclude that it is its consequence, namely
teacher attention, which, though negative in content, serves as
the reinforcement. While individual teachers will obviously
differ in how they act, one study showed that during a twenty
minute session appropriate behavior received teacher attention
an average of $1\frac{1}{5}$ times, while inappropriate behavior was
attended to an average of $8\frac{7}{10}$ times. In a different study the
records of observers revealed that teachers in the second and

third grades of an elementary school would reprimand disruptive children an average of five times per day, while during the same time the same children received less than one praise statement each.

Under these circumstances it is surprising that appropriate behavior does not disappear entirely with inappropriate behavior occurring all the time. The reason this does not happen is two-fold. For one, though a teacher's reprimand is a positive reinforcement for some children (it is better to be scolded than to be ignored altogether), it does not have that effect on everyone. For another, the occasional instance of teacher attention, together with the long-delayed reward for good work (the grade at the next marking period), are, fortunately, sufficient reinforcers for many children. These are the children who enter school already trained to work for delayed rewards or, to put it another way, who are able to postpone gratification.

Who Are These Children? The ability to postpone gratification, not to need constant rewards in order to keep on working, is one of the definitions of social maturity. Very young children must have their food the moment they feel hungry. Older children, especially in middle-class families, have learned to wait for their food until mealtime. We say that it is one of the characteristics of the immature adult to be unable to keep from snacking between meals. The ability to delay gratification thus seems to be something we acquire in the course of growing up, partly by virtue of our body's increased capacity to store nourishment, but largely because we are taught to "wait until later." In order for a child to learn this, two conditions must be present. One is that gratifiers are indeed available, and the other is that the person who says "wait until later" will, in fact, deliver the reward which has been promised.

We can see that learning to work for delayed rewards is more likely to occur in a family where things and experiences which can serve as rewards are available and where the adults who control these rewards are themselves stable, disciplined, and mature enough to keep the promises they make. On the other hand, a child who comes from a deprived, disorganized, unstable background is going to find it far more difficult to learn postponement of gratification. Following this reasoning, one might expect that the immature child or the child from a disadvantaged background will arrive at school ill-prepared to function under a system where good work is taken for granted while disruptive behavior is receiving most of the teacher's attention. It is not surprising, therefore, that in schools with a high percentage of children who come from deprived, disorganized homes, teachers encounter many highly disruptive children. They then spend most of their time correcting, scolding, and reprimanding only to find that the disruptive behavior stays pretty much at the same level or, in fact, increases over time.

It would be easy to blame the backgrounds of these children and to despair of the school's ever being able to accomplish anything constructive until the social problems in the community are solved. Without denying that these social problems demand solution at the highest level of priority, there is much the schools and the individual teacher in the schools can do in order to reverse the trend toward total disorganization. The teachers should identify the events which serve to strengthen behavior and arrange to have these events follow desired rather than undesired behavior. That means that if teacher attention increases the behavior which it follows, then attention ought to be "paid" for quiet, constructive, working behavior and not to disruptive, nonproductive behavior. (It is an interesting verbal convention that we speak of attention as something that is *paid*. Could it be that this expresses our awareness of the fact that attention is a powerful, positive reinforcer?)

What Teachers Notice. The effectiveness of using teacher attention as a reinforcer for desirable classroom behavior has been demonstrated in a great variety of schools and with a great variety of children. One of the most convincing of these demonstrations took place in 1966 in an elementary school in a university town in Illinois. This study focused on ten disruptive children in five classes whose teachers had participated in a seminar where the principles of behavior influence and behavior change had been explained. The children in question were selected by the teachers and the investigators. They were children who engaged in a great deal of behavior that interfered with classroom learning. This behavior included such activities as running around the room, starting fights with other children, talking out of turn, clapping hands, rattling paper, and destroying the property of others.

Trained observers watched these children and recorded their behavior before any intervention was begun. During this five-week period, the children were engaging in disruptive behavior an average of 62 percent of the time. Concurrently, the teachers were kept busy scolding, correcting, and reprimanding, leaving them relatively little time for instruction and less for praising and rewarding desirable behavior. At this point, the teachers were instructed to introduce the method to be evaluated. They were given three rules to follow. First, they were to make explicit to the children at the beginning of each period just what was expected of them, both in terms of behavior and of performance. The children were to be reminded of these rules whenever necessary during the class period. Next, the teachers were to ignore all behavior which interfered with learning or teaching, unless a child was being hurt by another. If punishment became necessary, it was to take the form of deprivation of some privilege, that is, a withdrawal of some positive reinforcer. Last and most importantly, the teachers were to give praise and attention to all behavior which served to further learning. In other words, the learning-incompatible behaviors, which had up to then been given so much teacher attention, were to be ignored, while the learning-appropriate behaviors, which had up to that point· been largely ignored, were now to be given attention. It is what psychologists call a reversal of contingencies.

The teachers were also told that they should attempt to reinforce the behaviors which were incompatible with those they wished to see decrease. Thus, since sitting quietly in one's seat and working is mutually exclusive with walking around the room and not working, the former was to be praised and the latter ignored. Examples of praise statements were given to the teachers ("I like the way you are working quietly"), and they were instructed to give praise for achievement, for socially constructive behavior, and for following the group rules which had been announced.

Almost as soon as these new methods were put into effect,

the disruptive behavior of all but one of the ten children showed a marked change for the better. One of the children did not improve very much until he was given tutoring in reading. That very week his behavior also began to show marked improvement. Obviously, if you can't do the work, you can't earn much praise, and being praised solely for sitting still is not enough. At any rate, for the ten children in the five classes who had shown an average of 62 percent disruptive behavior, the average disruptive behavior during the nine week period when the experimental method was in effect (and while the observers were counting) had fallen to 29 percent. All the children showed less troublesome behavior during that period, and each of the teachers had been able to put the new method of supporting desirable behavior to use. What is more, the other children in the classes were also reported to have "settled down," even though only the most disruptive had been the focus of the study. The *proper* use of teacher attention can, apparently, go a long way to solving some of the most troublesome classroom problems that interfere with what school is all about: learning.

A MOTHER'S LETTER

Dear Doctor,

I don't know whether you remember me but you saw me and my boy, Harry, three years ago when we had all that trouble with his school behavior. Harry has just completed sixth grade at the top of his class, and I thought you might be interested to hear that. Back when he was in the third grade we used to get telephone calls from the school almost once a week, telling us that Harry was acting up, "disrupting the class," as they called it. My husband and I made several trips to the school for conferences with the teachers, the psychologist, and the principal, all of whom told us that they thought Harry had some kind of emotional problem and that we should get help for him.

We couldn't understand why Harry should be such a problem at school when at home he seemed like a perfectly healthy and happy boy who was no more of a problem than any active youngster his age can be expected to be. Why should this child be speaking out of turn in class, getting out of his chair when he was not supposed to, and making noises that bothered the teacher and the other children? Because we were so puzzled, we took Harry to our pediatrician. She examined him but couldn't find anything wrong. She thought that if Harry was really such a problem in school, she might prescribe some kind of medicine for him, but she recommended that we wait awhile to see what would happen when he got into the fourth grade with different teachers.

But fourth grade was still six months away, and at the next marking period, a note on Harry's report card threatened that he might not get promoted. It was just then that we heard your talk at the PTA meeting of our older son's junior high school. You spoke about the classroom management procedures that were being studied at the university and how this showed that rewarding children for good behavior worked better than punishing them for bad behavior. When we talked to you briefly after your speech you gave us an appointment to see you at your office.

I still thank my lucky stars that we had gone to that PTA meeting that night. I'd hate to think what might have become of Harry if we had not learned about the behavior management approach. It is silly for me to tell you what you did because you must know that better than I. You got in touch with Harry's school and arranged to have one of your students observe what was going on in the classroom. Thank goodness the principal and his teacher were so cooperative.

As you explained the plan to us and Harry, the teacher would keep a record of Harry's good behavior and give him a card at the end of the day on which she would enter his good-behavior score for that day. When Harry got home, we would reward him with special privileges and special treats, depending on his score. It still seems to me that it worked like a miracle. Almost every day Harry's score would go up and I still recall, as if it had happened yesterday, when Harry came home three weeks after we had started the program and his card said in red letters, "A perfect day!" We had a real family party that day.

As I said at the beginning, my boy has just finished the sixth grade with a report card that said that he was the best student in the class. We have had no more trouble about his behavior and, needless to say, he continues to be a happy, outgoing child with many friends and numerous little hobbies and interests. I hope you are as pleased to hear that as I am pleased to tell you.

Very truly yours,
(Mrs.) Millie K.

If You Must Scold, At Least Don't Shout! It is the unusual teacher who spends more time praising than reprimanding, and constant reprimands are a very self-defeating way of maintaining so-called classroom discipline. Even the way the reprimands are delivered turns out to be wrong. When a teacher scolds a child, it is usually done in a loud voice so that the rest of the class can also hear it. Since it has been demonstrated that such loud reprimands serve to maintain and even to increase the very behavior the teacher wishes to decrease, the question arises whether a different way of reprimanding might be more effective.

Obviously not all teachers can change their own behavior overnight from scolding the disruptive to praising the constructive behavior. Furthermore, there are unacceptable behaviors, such as hitting other children, using profanities, or destroying property, which teachers simply cannot ignore. Not only that, but it is a well-established fact that when a behavior which has been receiving regular attention (or any other positive reinforcement) is suddenly ignored as the contingencies are reversed, such behavior will at first increase in frequency before it undergoes the gradual decline we call extinction. In a way it is as if the child, used to getting attention for his disruptive behavior and now finding this behavior ignored, redoubles his effort to gain attention by increasing the disruptiveness. Only when he finds that this gets him nowhere and that attention can be had for behaving constructively will such a child begin to substitute constructive for disruptive behavior.

At any rate, most teachers will need to have some form of

reprimand available in order to bridge the period between their use of the old mode of attending to the unacceptable behavior and the new way of attending to the desirable alternatives. One such substitute for the loud reprimand may be the soft reprimand. The feasibility of soft reprimands has been investigated with rather surprising results. Not only can they be substituted for loud reprimands, but they are, in fact, more effective than loud reprimands as a means of reducing disruptive classroom behavior. We shall first look at the details of one such study and then ask why it is that a whispered reprimand is better than one that is shouted.

When one wishes to investigate the effect of an intervention that is introduced into a classroom, such as a change from the use of loud reprimands to the use of soft reprimands in dealing with disruptive behavior, one runs into the question of how to be sure that any changes observed in child behavior are indeed the consequences of the change in the teacher's behavior. Could it be, for example, that the presence of the necessary observers in the classroom, or the change in subject matter being taught, or an approaching holiday, or simply the passing of time, brought about the reduction in disruptive behavior? The use of a control group, as in a typical scientific experiment, is often not feasible in classroom research because one cannot treat two halves of the children in a classroom differently (since one half would notice what was happening to the other half). Using two different classrooms is complicated by the fact that no two teachers and no two classrooms are sufficiently alike to permit meaningful comparisons. Short of the expensive use of very large numbers of teachers, classrooms, and children with random assignment of methods and other sophisticated experimental safeguards, one must devise a different way of making sure that one's conclusions are valid. One alternative is known as a reversal design.

Here one observes the behavior of interest under the typical conditions that prevailed before the experimenter came on the scene. In the case of the reprimand study, the frequency of disruptive behavior under the conditions of teachers giving out loud reprimands is counted. After a period of time that is long enough (usually three to four weeks) so that the presence of the observers is no longer a source of interest to the children, the experimenter introduces the change that is being investigated, in this instance, the regimen of soft reprimands. Again one lets three to four weeks pass, while the observation continues. By then, it should be apparent whether the introduction of the soft reprimand made a difference in terms of disruptive behavior. But, if the disruptive behavior did decrease in frequency, was that due to the soft reprimands or to something else? The answer can only be found by once again instituting the original (loud reprimand) condition and continuing the observations. If the change was due to the change in the loudness of reprimands, the rate of disruptive behaviors should go back up. If it does, one can then be fairly certain that an effective means of decreasing disruptive behavior has been found. Further certainty can be gained by the obvious step of returning to the soft-reprimand condition in order to test whether the disruptive behavior goes back down.

This reversal design has been used to investigate the effect of loud versus soft reprimands. It did indeed demonstrate that when teachers are able to follow the instructions to replace loud by soft reprimands, the disruptive classroom behavior decreased significantly.

Not every teacher in the study we have just discussed was able to switch readily from loud to soft reprimands. Soft reprimands require that the teacher walk over to the child who is misbehaving and quietly indicate disapproval. One teacher viewed this as a sign of weakness; apparently it is a sign of a strong teacher to be able to shout. Having to walk over to the offending child requires more energy than standing in front of the class and yelling, and as the day wears on and the teacher gets tired and irritated, yelling seems far easier. On the other hand, teachers who were able to use soft reprimands consistently soon discovered that they had fewer occasions for giving out reprimands as the children's behavior improved. Thus, we can conclude that soft reprimands, especially when combined with consistent praise for desirable behavior, are a very effective means of improving classroom behavior.

Why should this be the case? The answer is not known but one can venture some speculations. The major differences between loud and soft reprimands are the teacher's voice level and the teacher's proximity to the child receiving the repri-

mand. When the rest of the class can hear a child being reprimanded, something seems to happen both to that child and to
the rest of the students. That something may well be a degree of
excitement. A shouting teacher is—or at least appears to be—
more angry than a whispering teacher. Anger in others tends to
agitate those who observe it, and the vicious cycle where loud
reprimands result in more and more disruptive behavior has
often been observed and might support this speculation. Furthermore, a child who is being yelled at may be viewed, in
some fashion, as a victim with whom the rest of the class
sympathizes and this sympathy from the peers may be, for that
child, more rewarding than the teacher's reprimand is punishing. This peer-generated reward is lost when the teacher whis-
pers a reprimand. Thus, when praise statements are announced
loudly and reprimands delivered quietly, the effect seems to be
that desirable behavior of the entire class increases, with a
concomitant decrease in disruptive behavior.

Although the exception does not necessarily prove the rule,
it can often help us to sharpen our understanding of the rule.
One of the children in the reprimand study we have been
discussing became more disruptive under the soft-reprimand
condition. For him it was apparently reinforcing to have the
teacher come over to his desk, lean down, and whisper, "Harry,
don't do that." This exception underscores an important principle which, though we have stated it before, bears emphasizing
again: There are no universal reinforcers. If we want our teaching to be as effective as possible, we must ascertain for each and
every child what reinforces and what does not and act accordingly. Assumptions of what should work or generalizations
based on our own preferences are very poor guides. Only
observations of what actually happens can provide us with a
valid and usable basis for working with children. It is likely that
the teachers we call sensitive, intuitive, and effective are those
who are able to make these observations and to act in accordance with them. In turn, the superiority of individualized
teaching over mass education probably rests on the fact that
effectiveness is maximized when each student not only is presented with appropriate material but also encounters the consequences for performance that are effective reinforcers for him or
her at that moment.

We do not have all the answers to effective teaching and constructive classroom management, but we have a lot of knowledge that begs to be put to use. What we need in education is less reliance on speculative theories and on pronouncements by self-appointed authorities and more trust in our own observations and the facts these observations reveal.

SUMMING UP

In the preface to this book I spoke of my desire to tell parents, teachers, and others who care about children some of the things I, as a psychologist, know about learning disabilities and other school-related problems. Through this sharing of knowledge— this giving psychology away—I wanted to suggest some ways in which the science of human behavior might be put to use by those who live and work with troubled children.

While I expressed the hope of being able to offer some helpful ideas, I also warned that the knowledge psychologists have to offer is still tentative and incomplete. I pointed out that we have developed some general principles which can be applied to improve learning and to change behavior, but I also said that these principles have not yet achieved the status of scientific laws. Yet, the children about whom we care cannot wait until we psychologists are perfectly certain about our knowledge. We must try to deal with their problems now, not fifty years from now when we may have achieved certainty. Thus, the preceding pages were written in the spirit of doing the best we can while recognizing our limitations. Let us review some of the principal points which have been covered.

Labels Can Be Deceptive

A lot of children may be engaging in behavior that looks fairly much alike, but giving all of these children the same label, such as *learning disabled,* is often less than helpful. Labeling a problem is not a harmless exercise in classification. Labeling almost always leads to important consequences which may or may not benefit the child who has been given the label. Labels obscure important differences and thereby prevent us from coming to an understanding of the problems of the individual child. What is more, giving a problem a label often leads people to believe that the problem is explained when, in reality, the label only describes what one has observed, and explains nothing. If one observes that a child has trouble reading, ascribing that trouble to dyslexia is no more than expressing the observation in Greek. Furthermore, the label *dyslexia*, with its medical connotations, removes the responsibility for helping that child from the realm of education, where it ought to lie, and places it into the realm of medicine, where the teaching of reading does not belong.

In order to reduce the confusion about who should and who should not be called learning disabled, we proposed a definition which we can now restate:

> A learning-disabled child is a child of at least average intelligence whose academic performance is impaired by a developmental lag in the ability to sustain selective attention. Such a child requires specialized instruction in order to permit the use of his or her full intellectual potential.

It is the intent and implication of this definition that the problem of the learning-disabled child be viewed as falling squarely into the realm of education. Speculations about brain functions or brain dysfunctions are, for the most part, gratuitous. They don't aid the child who needs to be helped to learn.

Tests Don't Always Tell

A learning disability is manifested in a discrepancy between how well a child should be able to do in school and the performance that child is actually producing. How well a child should be able to do is essentially a question about that child's learning potential. But learning and learning potential are very difficult to measure. This is because learning is a process that cannot be observed directly and learning potential is an inference about something that lies in the future.

The best we can do is to seek a measure of the child's intelligence and to compare it with that child's school achievement. But tests of intelligence are no more than tests of current performance; they do not measure absolute intelligence and share with other tests of achievement a susceptibility to influences of experience, motivation, anxiety, and physical condition. For that reason, discrepancies between intelligence test scores and achievement test scores may reflect a great many things other than learning disability. The assessment of learning ability and the ascertaining of learning disability are very complicated tasks which should never be attempted on the basis of any one test or in any single testing session, no matter how experienced the evaluator.

Hyperactivity and Learning Disability Are Not Synonymous

Many learning-disabled children have trouble sitting still and many children who have trouble sitting still have difficulties in learning. It is not clear what is cause and what is effect in that relationship. What is clear is that the two phenomena are distinctly different, and that the hyperactive child needs help with learning to sit still while the learning-disabled child needs help with learning. Simply helping a child who is both learning disabled and hyperactive to sit still, whether by means of drugs or otherwise, will not do anything for that child's learning. Learning can only take place through teaching; it does not come out of a medicine bottle.

Attention Has Many Facets

When we say, "Jimmy, pay attention," what do we mean? Moreover, how do we know when Jimmy is paying attention? Like intelligence and learning, attention is a construct psychologists find useful in their work. But constructs are not things or entities which can be observed; their presence or absence can only be inferred by observing what people do. One aspect of attention that seems particularly relevant to the study of learning-disabled children is selectivity. It has to do with focusing on those aspects of a situation which are critical for coping with it in a constructive fashion. In reading, for example, we must focus on the printed material and on the shape, order, and relationship of the letters and words. The good reader is better than the poor reader on laboratory tests of selective attention. Studies of normal and of learning-disabled children suggest that selective attention is an ability which develops in the course of a child's growing up. A lag in the development of that ability may be a source of learning disability. Learning-disabled children may be children for whom there is a mismatch between their development and the way in which they are being taught. More careful matching between a child's ability to sustain selective attention and the teaching methods one uses might reduce the number of children we call learning disabled.

Learning-disabled Children Can Learn

If one adopts the position that learning-disabled children have not yet developed optimal selective attention, there emerge a number of ways of teaching them. One is to increase the distinctiveness of the differentiating aspects of stimuli, such as letters, which they are to learn to tell apart. Another is to let them experience things like letters through more than one sense modality, and in more than one version or form. We can maintain their attention to what we want them to notice by maintaining novelty and by rewarding them for doing what we want them to do. Moreover, we should teach them not only what to do but also how to do it. It is not enough to say, "Pay attention." One must show a child to what to attend and how to go about doing that. Above all, we must keep individual differences in mind. No one teaching or training method will work with every child, regardless of level of development, age, motivation, or stage of learning.

Strategies for Teaching Strategies of Learning

Teaching a child how to pay attention is a matter of teaching a strategy. Teaching such strategies can be done in several ways. One of these is by demonstration; another is by teaching children to give verbal instructions to themselves. In all this it is important to focus on the positive things the child is supposed to do, not on the negative things we wish to eliminate. The principle that behavior is a function of its consequences has many applications in the teaching of children. Rewards for desirable behavior are more effective, in the long run, than punishments for undesirable behavior. Our attention tends to be a powerful reinforcing reward for many children. Unfortunately, most of us tend to pay far more attention to the irritating and annoying things children do than to their constructive and pleasing behavior.

Learning Not to Go to School

We are all more likely to do that which is pleasant and rewarding than that which is unpleasant and painful. Children are no different. If staying home is more pleasant than going to school, there will be a strong tendency to remain at home. Many cases of school refusal may well start because a parent fails to insist that the child go to school, permitting the child to stay home and do pleasant things. The longer a child stays away from school, the harder it will be to return there, and eventually such a child may become school phobic. Prevention and early intervention are as important here as in most other problem areas. Few school-related cases are more difficult to treat than a fourteen- or fifteen-year-old adolescent who refuses to go to school.

Fighting Aggression

We devoted the last chapter to a discussion of the troublesome behavior we call aggression. We pointed out that like other responses, aggression can be learned. It can be strengthened or weakened, depending on the consequences which are forthcoming when one behaves in an aggressive manner. In theory, at least, it is possible to raise a nonaggressive child. Whether one wants to do this depends on one's values.

This point about values brings us back to something I said in the preface. Psychology can tell us how to influence behavior; it cannot tell us the direction such influences should take. That depends on our values. Those seeking to influence the behavior of a child must scrupulously examine their values. The same psychological principles that permit one to teach a child to be honest can also be used to teach the child to be a liar. Here the choice seems easy. How about the choice between having children obey their teacher and having them question the teacher's decisions? That choice is not easy. But in our time it is not easy to be a parent, nor to be a teacher, nor, indeed, to be a child. That will not change, no matter what knowledge psychologists might have to give away.

ANNOTATED REFERENCES

The following references permit the reader to explore various topics in greater depth. Citations are listed in the order in which the relevant subject is mentioned in the chapters. Research studies mentioned in the text are here identified with their bibliographic references. The more technical books and journals can usually be found in college and university libraries or obtained through them on interlibrary loan. General public libraries are unlikely to have these items in their collections.

Chapter 1

Ross, A. O. *Psychological aspects of learning diabilities and reading disorders.* New York: McGraw-Hill, 1976. This work contains a more technical discussion of many of the issues raised in this and the following chapters.

Chapter 2

Goldstein, K. *Aftereffects of brain-injuries in war.* New York: Grune & Stratton, 1942. A translation of an earlier German edition, describing Goldstein's pioneering work and presenting his conclusions about the functions of the brain.

Werner, H., & Strauss, A. A. Pathology of figure-background relation in the child. *Journal of Abnormal and Social Psychology,* 1941, **36**, 236–248. One of the papers reflecting the product of the collaboration of these pioneers.

Strauss, A. A., & Lehtinen, L. E. *Psychopathology and education of the brain-injured child.* New York: Grune & Stratton, 1947. A highly influential book which grew out of Strauss' earlier work with Werner.

Cruickshank, W. M. *The brain injured child in home, school, and community.* Syracuse, N.Y.: Syracuse University Press, 1967. A book which reflects the earlier work of this important contributor to the field.

Kephart, N. C. *The slow learner in the classroom* (2d ed.). Columbus, Ohio: Merrill, 1971. When the first edition of this book appeared in 1960, it was unique in its concrete recommendations of how the teacher might deal with the "slow learner."

Johnson, D. J., & Myklebust, H. R. *Learning disabilities: Educational principles and practices.* New York: Grune & Stratton, 1967. This text reflects Myklebust's psychoneurological approach which was so strongly influenced by his earlier work with the deaf.

Chapter 3

Stevenson, H. W. *Children's learning.* New York: Appleton-Century-Crofts, 1972. A highly authoritative, technical discussion of what psychologists know about this topic.

Rosenthal, R., & Jacobson, L. *Pygmalion in the classroom.* New York: Holt, Rinehart & Winston, 1968. This book presented the much publicized research findings that teachers' work with a child can be influenced by what they believe about that child's potential.

Chapter 4

Routh, D. K., & Roberts, R. D. Minimal brain dysfunction in children. Failure to find evidence for a behavioral syndrome. *Psychological Reports,* 1972, **31**, 307–314. This study, conducted at the University of Iowa, is one of several which show that the various problems of so-called MBD children do not "hang together" to form a syndrome.

Crinella, F. M. Identification of brain dysfunction syndromes in children through profile analysis: Patterns associated with so-called "minimal brain dysfunction." *Journal of Abnormal Psychology,* 1973, **82**, 33–45. Learning-disabled children and children with known brain lesions are quite unlike one another.

Clements, S. D. *Minimal brain dysfunction in children.* NINDB Monograph #3 (USPHS Publication #1415). Washington, D.C.: U.S. Department of Health, Education, & Welfare, 1966. A government sponsored attempt to make sense out of the notion of minimal brain dysfunction. It includes the list of 99 problems.

Stewart, M. A., & Olds, S. W. *Raising a hyperactive child.* New York: Harper & Row, 1972. A sensible approach to children whose primary problem is their excessive activity level.

Feingold, B. F. *Why your child is hyperactive.* New York: Random House, 1975. Raises the intriguing question whether some forms of hyperactivity might be due to reactions to food additives and food coloring.

Wender, P. H. *Minimal brain dysfunction in children.* New York: Wiley, 1971. An example of the more extreme advocacy of drugs as the principal mode of treatment for hyperactive children.

Ellis, M. J., Witt, P. A., Reynolds, R., & Sprague, R. L. Methylphenidate and the activity of hyperactives in the informal setting. *Child Development,* 1974, **45**, 217–220. This is one of a series of studies conducted at the University of Illinois under the general direction of Dr. Sprague which examines the relationship between drug dosage, hyperactivity, and learning.

Chapter 5

Cronbach, L. J. Five decades of public controversy over mental testing. *American Psychologist,* 1975, **30**, 1–14. An authoritative statement of many of the issues involved in assessing intelligence.

Wechsler, D. *Wechsler Intelligence Scale for Children—Revised.* New York: The Psychological Corp., 1974. The manual for this test contains a discussion of the definition of intelligence, as viewed by this pioneer in the field of testing.

Kirk, S. A., McCarthy, J. J., & Kirk, W. D. *Illinois Test of Psycholinguistic Abilities* (rev. ed.). Urbana, Ill.: University of Illinois Press, 1968. The basic reference for the ITPA. Like other test manuals, the circulation of this one is restricted to professional readers in order to safeguard the validity of the test.

Anderson, W. F. The relative effects of the Frostig program, corrective reading instruction, and attention upon the reading skills of corrective readers with visual perceptual difficulties. *Journal of School Psychology,* 1972, **10**, 387–395. Reports a study which compared the Frostig program with other approaches and found that it did not live up to the claims made for it by its authors.

Chapter 6

Hallahan, D. P. Distractibility in the learning-disabled child. In W. M. Cruickshank & D. P. Hallahan (Eds.), *Perceptual and learning disabilities in children.* Syracuse, N.Y.: Syracuse University Press, 1975. Vol. 2. Pp. 195–218. A summary of research on the topics mentioned in this chapter.

Vande Voort, L., Senf, G. M., & Benton, A. L. Development of audiovisual integration in normal and retarded readers. *Child Development,* 1972, **43**, 1260–1272. Reports a research study based on the method of signal detection.

Satz, P., Rardin, D., & Ross, J. An evaluation of a theory of specific developmental dyslexia. *Child Development,* 1971, **42**, 2009–2021. A study of selective attention, using the method of dichotic listening.

Hallahan, D. P., Kauffman, J. M., & Ball, D. W. Effects of stimulus attenuation on selective attention performance of children. *Journal of Genetic Psychology*, 1974, **125**, 71–77. Demonstrates that it is possible to improve selective attention of children.

Hallahan, D. P., & Kauffman, J. M. Research on the education of distractible and hyperactive children. In W. M. Cruickshank & D. P. Hallahan (Eds.), *Perceptual and learning disabilities in children*. Syracuse, N.Y.: Syracuse University Press, 1975. Vol. 2. Pp. 221–256. An authoritative summary of recent research, including studies cited in this chapter. The authors are among the most productive scientists in this field.

Hagen, J. W., & Hale, G. A. The development of attention in children. In A. D. Pick (Ed.), *Minnesota Symposium on Child Psychology*. Vol. 7. Minneapolis, Minn.: University of Minnesota Press, 1973. Pp. 117–140. A basic reference on the developmental changes in children's attention.

Hale, G. A., & Morgan, J. S. Developmental trends in children's component selection. *Journal of Experimental Child Psychology*, 1973, **15**, 302–314. A further demonstration of developmental changes in selective attention.

Sroufe, L. A., Sonies, B. C., West, W. D., & Wright, F. S. Anticipatory heart rate deceleration and reaction time in children with and without referral for learning disability. *Child Development*, 1973, **44**, 267–273. These investigators used heart rate as a measure of attention and showed that learning-disabled children differed from normal controls.

Salapatek, P., & Kessen, W. Prolonged investigation of a plane geometric triangle by the human infant. *Journal of Experimental Child Psychology*, 1973, **15**, 22–29. Even in infants one can find individual differences in the deployment of attention.

Caron, A. J. Conceptual transfer in preverbal children as a consequence of dimensional training. *Journal of Experimental Child Psychology*, 1968, **6**, 522–542. A study which demonstrated that even very young children can be taught to make difficult discriminations.

Koenigsberg, R. S. An evaluation of visual versus sensorimotor methods for improving orientation discrimination for letter reversal by preschool children. *Child Development*, 1973, **44**, 764–769. Another demonstration that attention can be improved through training and that this may be the "active ingredient" in so-called visual-motor training programs.

Wheeler, R. J., & Dusek, J. B. The effects of attentional and cognitive factors on children's incidental learning. *Child Development*, 1973, **44**, 253–258. The nature of training must take the child's developmental level into account.

Chapter 7

Palkes, H., Stewart, M., & Kahana, B. Porteus maze performance of hyperactive boys after training in self-directed verbal commands. *Child Develop-*

ment, 1968, **39**, 817–829. Details of the "stop-look-and-listen" study can be found in this reference.

Meichenbaum, D. H., & Goodman, J. Training impulsive children to talk to themselves: A means of developing self-control. *Journal of Abnormal Psychology*, 1971, **77**, 115–126. A much cited study which showed the importance of teaching children the strategies for solving problems.

Egeland, B. Training impulsive children in the use of more efficient scanning techniques. *Child Development*, 1974, **45**, 165–171. Another demonstration of the superiority of teaching a strategy over telling children to take their time in working on a problem.

Ross, A. O. *Psychological disorders of children: A behavioral approach to theory, research, and therapy*. New York: McGraw-Hill, 1974. Contains details of the behavioral approach to helping children who have psychological problems.

Patterson, G. R., Jones, R., Whittier, J., & Wright, M. A. A behavior modification technique for the hyperactive child. *Behaviour Research and Therapy*, 1965, **2**, 217–226. The source for the case of "Raymond."

O'Leary, K. D., & O'Leary, S. G. (Eds.). *Classroom management: The successful use of behavior modification*. New York: Pergamon Press, 1972. A collection of studies on classroom management. Includes a chapter detailing how behavior principles can be implemented by a teacher.

McKenzie, H. S., Clark, M., Wolf, M. M., Kothera, R., & Benson, C. Behavior modification of children with learning disabilities using grades as tokens and allowances as back-up reinforcers. *Exceptional Children*, 1968, **34**, 745–752. Reference to the study on this topic cited in the text.

Hawkins, R. P., Sluyter, D. J., & Smith, C. D. Modification of achievement by a simple technique involving parents and teacher. In M. Harris (Ed.), *Classroom uses of behavior modification*. Columbus, Ohio: Merrill, 1972. Pp. 101–120. A study, conducted in Michigan, in which a token program involved cooperation between the home and the school.

Chapter 8

Kennedy, W. A. School phobia: Rapid treatment of fifty cases. *Journal of Abnormal Psychology*, 1965, **70**, 285–289. A persuasive presentation of the successful use of early intervention.

Garvey, W. P., & Hegrenes, J. R. Desensitization techniques in the treatment of school phobia. *American Journal of Orthopsychiatry*, 1966, **36**, 147–152. Describes the use of gradually increasing the child's proximity to school in a form of systematic desensitization.

Chapter 9

Walters, R. H. On the high-magnitude theory of aggression. *Child Development*, 1964, **35**, 303–304. A statement of this theory by one of its authors.

Davitz, J. L. The effects of previous training on postfrustration behavior. *Journal of Abnormal and Social Psychology*, 1952, **47**, 309–315. A demonstration that responses to frustration can be learned and that aggression is only one of these responses.

Patterson, G. R., Littman, R. A., & Bricker, W. Assertive behavior in children: A step toward a theory of aggression. *Monographs of the Society for Research in Child Development*, 1967, **32**, 5. (Whole No. 113). A report on an extended study of young children which demonstrated that aggression is learned when it "pays off."

Bandura, A., & Walters, R. H. *Adolescent aggression*. New York: Ronald, 1959. The classic work in which aggression is analyzed from the point of view of social learning theory and containing a report on a study which showed that parents who punish the aggressive behavior of their children, raise children who are aggressive.

Walters, R. H., & Brown, M. Studies of reinforcement of aggression: III. Transfer of responses to an interpersonal situation. *Child Development*, 1963, **34**, 563–571. Children who are rewarded for hitting a punching bag will later hit other children.

Mallick, S. K., & McCandless, B. R. A study of catharsis of aggression. *Journal of Personality and Social Psychology*, 1966, **4**, 591–596. An adult's permissive attitude toward aggression leads to further aggression, and getting aggressive feelings "out of one's system" is not the answer to reducing children's aggression.

Skinner, B. F. *Science and human behavior*. New York: Macmillan, 1953. The classic statement on the application of reinforcement principles to human behavior.

Hall, R. V., Lund, D., & Jackson, D. Effects of teacher attention on study behavior. *Journal of Applied Behavior Analysis*, 1968, **1**, 1–12. When teachers attend to disruptive behavior and not to desired behavior, disruptive behavior is reinforced and increases in frequency.

Madsen, C. H., Becker, W. C., & Thomas, D. R. Rules, praise, and ignoring: Elements of elementary classroom control. *Journal of Applied Behavior Analysis*, 1968, **1**, 139–150. Demonstrated the differential teacher attention devoted to appropriate versus inappropriate behavior.

Becker, W. C., Madsen, C. H., Arnold, C. R., & Thomas, D. R. The contingent use of teacher attention and praise in reducing classroom behavior problems. *The Journal of Special Education*, 1967, **1**, 287–307. The 1966 Illinois study cited in the text.

O'Leary, K. D., Kaufman, K. F., Kass, R. E., & Drabman, R. The effects of loud and soft reprimands on the behavior of disruptive children. *Exceptional Children*, 1970, **37**, 145–155. Reports that the typical teacher produces five reprimands but less than one praise per child per day, and demonstrates that soft reprimands are more effective than those which are shouted.

INDEX

Achievement tests, 42
Aggression, 163–172, 190
  and anger, 168
  catharsis of, 171
  definition of, 164
  as learned behavior, 169
Anderson, W. F., 194
Anxiety, 117
Arnold, C. R., 197
Attention, 80, 96–97
  aspects of, 188
  enhancement of, 119, 135
  as reinforcement, 177–179
  (*See also* Selective attention)
Autism (*see* Early infantile autism)
Ayllon, T., 154

Ball, D. W., 194
Bandura, A., 197
Becker, W. C., 197
Behavior, vacuum of, 136–137
Benson, C., 196
Benton, A. L., 194
Binet, A., 64
Brain damage, 12, 17–19
  results of, 19, 45–46
  (*See also* Minimal brain dysfunction)
Brain functions, 13
Bricker, W., 197
Brown, M., 197

Caron, A. J., 195
Catharsis of aggressive impulses, 171
Cause and effect, 52, 56
Cerebral palsy, 23
Clark, M., 196

Classroom problems, management of,
    173–185
Clements, S. D., 193
Component selection, 105–107
Construct validity, 102
Correlation and cause, 52
  (*See also* Cause and effect)
Crinella, F. M., 193
Cronbach, L. J., 194
Cruickshank, W. M., 23, 192

Davitz, J. L., 196
de Hirsch, K., 28
Desensitization to feared objects, 157
Development, 111–117
  changes in course of, 111
  differences in rate of, 111
  lag in, 111
    cumulative effect of, 117
Dichotic listening and reading
    problems, 103
Directionality, 24, 119
Disruptive children, 163, 175–177
Distinctive features, 118
Distractibility, 100
Drabman, R. S., 197
Drugs, 55–60
  abuses of, 60
  alternative for, 59
  attitudes toward, 59
  diagnostic uses of, 56
  effectiveness of, research on, 55
  effects of, 57
    attribution of, 59
    on learning, 57–58
Dusek, J. B., 195
Dyslexia, 6–7

Early infantile autism, 100, 112–113, 115
Egeland, B., 196
Electroencephalography (EEG), 49
Ellis, M. J., 194
Emotional problems, 9

Failure, fear of, 148
Familial defectives, 8
Fears, 148, 151–152
Feingold, B. F., 193
Frostig, M., 26, 27, 91
Frostig Developmental Test of Visual Perception, 25–26, 91–92
Frustration, 167

Garmezy, N., *xiv*
Garvey, W. P., 196
Gestalt psychology, 18, 21
Getman, G., 25
Goldstein, K., 15–21, 28, 192
Goodman, J., 195
Grades as reinforcers, 138, 140
Gratification, postponement of, 176

Hagen, J. W., 195
Hale, G. A., 195
Hall, R. V., 197
Hallahan, D. P., 194, 195
Hawkins, R. P., 196
Heart rate, 107
Hegrenes, J. R., 196
History of learning disability area, 15–28
Home-based treatment, 138
Hyperactive child, remedial work with, 128–130
Hyperactivity, 49–55, 127
    and brain damage, 51
    effects of drugs on, 55
    and learning disabilities, 49, 51, 188
Hyperkinesis (*see* Hyperactivity)
Hypothetical construct, 65

Illinois Test of Psycholinguistic Abilities (ITPA), 26, 80–91
Impulse, control of, 131

Impulsivity, 49, 100, 132
    as learned response style, 132
    reduction of, 131
Incidental learning, 104–105
    developmental changes in, 105
Intelligence, 40, 64–66
    test of, 64–67
    test performance, 41, 67, 77
        interpretation of, 75–80
Intelligence quotient (IQ), 64, 75
Intervention:
    behavioral methods of, 133–137
    cognitive methods of, 128–132
    goal of, 126–127
ITPA (Illinois Test of Psycholinguistic Abilities), 26, 80–91

Jackson, D., 197
Jacobson, L., 193
James, W., 46
Johnson, D. J., 193
Jones, R., 196

Kahana, B., 195
Kass, R. E., 197
Kauffman, J. M., 194, 195
Kaufman, K. F., 197
Kennedy, W. A., 155–157, 196
Kephart, N. C., 22, 24, 25, 27, 193
Kessen, W., 195
Kirk, S. A., 26–27, 81, 92, 194
Kirk, W. D., 81, 194
Koenigsberg, R. S., 195
Kothera, R., 196

Labeling, 4, 7, 186–187
Language, 27–28, 81, 82
Laterality, 24, 118
Learning, 29–43
    capacity for, 34
    definition of, 32
    measures of, 35
Learning disability:
    cause of, 5, 111, 115–117
    definition of, 5, 8–12, 36–39
    description of, 4
    prevention of, 117
    research on, 94–96

Learning disability *(Cont.)*:
  tests of, 90–92
  treatment of, 124–144, 189
Lehtinen, L. E., 22, 192
Lesson refusal, 159–162
Littman, R. A., 197
Lund, D., 197

McCandless, B. R., 197
McCarthy, J. J., 194
McKenzie, H. S., 196
Madsen, C. H., 197
Mallick, S. K., 197
Matching Familiar Figures test, 132
MBD *(see* Minimal brain dysfunction)
Medication *(see* Drugs)
Meichenbaum, D. H., 195
Mental retardation, 8, 19–20
Methylphenidate *(see* Ritalin)
Miller, G. A., *xiii*
Minimal brain dysfunction (MBD), 14,
    45, 47, 48
  symptoms of, 49
Modeling of behavior, 130, 171
Morgan, J. S., 195
Myklebust, H. R., 28, 193

Nonaggressive children, 172–173

Olds, S. W., 193
O'Leary, K. D., 196, 197
O'Leary, S. G., 196
Osgood, C., 27
Overexclusive attention, 112
Overinclusive attention, 113

Palkes, H., 195
Parents, participation of, in treatment
    program, 137–142
Patterson, G. R., 196, 197
Peers as reinforcers, 135
Perceptual-motor disturbances, 21, 49
Perceptual-motor training, 22
  efficacy of, 91
Placebo, 55

Potential, 40–41
  and achievement, 39, 81
  measurement of, 40
Praise, 123, 140, 160
Prevention of learning disabilities, 117
Psychotherapy, 157, 171
Punishment, 133–134, 161–162, 170

Rardin, D., 194
Reinforcement, 133, 142
  back-up, 141
  grades and, 138, 140
  peers and, 135
  social, 123, 140, 160
  token, 139
Reprimand:
  loud versus soft, 181–184
  as reinforcer, 175, 181
Reversal in reading, 1, 99
Rewards, 120, 160–161
  (See also Reinforcement)
Reynolds, R., 194
Ritalin, 55, 107
  (See also Drugs)
Roberts, R. D., 193
Rogers, M., 154
Rosenthal, R., 193
Ross, A. O., 192, 196
Ross, J., 194
Routh, D. K., 193

Salapatek, P., 195
Satz, P., 194
School phobia, 147–152
  prevention of, 148–151
  sex differences in, 150
  treatment of, 155–158
School refusal, 145–147, 190
Selective attention, 80, 96–123
  development of, 111–117
  developmental changes in, 114–117
  enhancement of, 118–122
  and learning, 97–100
  and learning disability, 101–107, 111,
    117
  and performance, 100–101
  and reading, 80
  rewards for, 120
  and school performance, 100–101

Self-command, 129
Self-control, training in, 129
Self-instructions, teaching, 128–132
Senf, G. M., 194
Signal detection, 102
Skinner, B. F., 175, 197
Sluyter, D. J., 196
Smith, C. D., 196
Smith, D., 154
Social reinforcement, 123, 140, 160
Socioeconomic status, 43, 176
Soldiers, brain injuries sustained by, 15–19
Sonies, B. C., 195
Sprague, R. L., 194
Sroufe, L. A., 195
Stevenson, H. W., 193
Stewart, M. A., 193, 195
Stimulus-bound responding, 17, 20, 106
Strategy for responding, 121
  of good readers, 122
  teaching of, 121–122, 189
Strauss, A. A., 19–24, 27, 192

Taylor, E. M., 46
Teaching matched to child's capacity, 121–123
Television, violence on, 172

Tests, psychological 25–27, 61–93, 187–188
  (See also specific test)
Thomas, D. R., 197
Token program, 139–144
Token reinforcement, 139
Truancy, 145–147

Validity, 86
Vande Voort, L., 194
Visual-motor coordination, 119
Visual perception, 26, 91–92

Walters, R. H., 196, 197
Wechsler, D., 65, 194
Wechsler Intelligence Scale for
      Children, Revised (WISC-R), 65, 67–80
Wender, P. H., 193
Werner, H., 19–21, 192
West, W. D., 195
Wheeler, R. J., 195
Whittier, J., 196
Witt, P. A., 194
Wolf, M. M., 196
Wright, F. S., 195
Wright, M. A., 196